Religion and Human Experience

Religion
and Human
experience

by Andrew Panzarella, FSC

ST. MARY'S COLLEGE PRESS • Winona, Minnesota

Illustrations by Anna Maria Ahl

First Printing, December 1974
Second Printing, July 1975

ISBN 0-88489-058-9

Library of Congress Card Catalog #73-87024

Religion and Human Experience

© 1974 by St. Mary's College Press, Winona, Minnesota

CONTENTS

PREFACE

For over a hundred years two statues have stood by the main entrance to the University of Paris. They seem to be students of long ago who were struck immobile on their way home from a lecture. Now they silently challenge everyone who enters. The statue on the left side of the doorway clutches a book firmly with both hands, holds his head up very high, and solemnly stares out over the busy street. The statue on the right side of the doorway is on the verge of dropping the book dangling from his left hand while his right hand can barely keep his puzzled face from falling into the folds of his cape. The reader who can imagine this scene as he opens the first pages of this book will find himself challenged too. Does he expect to find here the kind of knowledge that will enable him to look out over the busy world like someone who possesses the answers? Or does he expect to find the kind of knowledge that will make him look within himself like someone who is possessed by the questions? Hopefully, a little bit of both.

Although we are living at a time when the institutions of religion seem to be faltering, we are aware of the peculiarity that at the same time personal religion seems to be moving toward a renaissance. The intensifying interest in personal religion is evident in the Jesus movement, in the quest for mystical experiences that lies behind the popularity of Eastern religion, meditation, and some drug cultures, and also in the new search for values. It parallels the new interest in man. After having acquired the ability to make sweeping transformations in the world around him, man is asking what he can do to transform himself. The young science of psychology had barely begun to discover what man is when people started asking what man could become. It is this preoccupation with the human potential that has brought renewed interest in personal religion.

Since psychology has assigned itself the work of studying man, people look to psychology for answers to their questions about man and man's possibilities. There are limits to the answers psychology can give. Particularly when we ask about the human potential, we are asking questions which are far ahead of our answers. Yet it is reasonable to expect some information about what we are and some clues to what we can become. The role of religion in human behavior has been of interest to a small number of psychologists over the years, though it must be admitted that the early psychologists tended to take a rather negative attitude towards religion on the whole. But recently, as the emphasis has begun shifting from what man is to what man can become, a more positive view of religion has emerged in psychological circles. Psychology is in a better position today to present a balanced view of how religion and human goals can interact.

This small book attempts to summarize in a non-technical way some of the information and some of the new questions that have arisen in the study of religion and human personality. The findings do not always favor religion. Nor do they always disfavor religion. Instead, they make us more sophisticated. We begin to realize that there are a variety of religious outlooks, some of which lead to greater human fulfillment and others to psychological immaturity. In this book both kinds of religious outlooks, the fulfilling and the infantilizing, will be considered. It is necessary to examine both kinds of religious outlooks if one is going to chart a course for human and religious fulfillment.

When the reader is filtering the following pages through his own mind and judging them in the light of his own experience of life, he may benefit by knowing something about the author who has selected these materials and passed so many judgments in presenting them. The author is a professional religious, a member of The Brothers of the Christian Schools. He is also a professional psychologist. Hence, he has been deeply involved with both religion and psychology. His personal experience as a religious has led him to concentrate more on the humanistic aspects of psychology, which include the psychology of personal meaning, of growth, of moral development, of ecstasy, and of social relations. His personal experience as a psychologist has led him to emphasize how individual each person is and how different religion can be for each person.

Chapter 1

Religious Development: Childhood to Maturity

European literature of a few centuries ago suggests that most mothers at that time did not love their babies. Those who did were cautioned not to love them too much. Only one child out of five survived to the age of five, so that loving an infant was taking a great emotional risk. Though medical science has removed most of the risk in Western countries today, the human infant is still among the most fragile creatures on earth. Most animals by the time they are a year old are fully grown, capable of surviving on their own, and reproducing. But even under the best conditions a human being remains practically helpless for several years before he can function adequately on his own. The structure of the nervous system and brain takes fifteen years to mature fully. The body takes more than twenty years for full development. The education and experience necessary to survive comfortably in contemporary Western society take still longer.

The Process of Religious Growth

Development is fragmented, uneven, and uncertain in a human being. Since the human is more complex than other organisms and has a wider range of possibilities open to him, it is understandable that his development takes longer and may be more segmented. Some segments of an individual's personality may be very developed while others are still infantile. An accomplished engineer may have a highly developed mind for physics and mathematics but the mind of a grammar school child for politics or art or human relations. The world of human beings is so complex that it is common for persons to be highly developed in many ways while remaining relatively undeveloped in other respects. One area in which many people tend to remain on an immature level is religion. It is not unusual to find people who have experienced much of life, and well educated people too, who have remained at a childhood level in their religious development. Immersed in the practicalities of their everyday life and work, they have not taken the time for religious learning, reflection, and development. Their religious development may have nearly ended in childhood or adolescence.

It may be difficult to accept the statement that a person should not remain a child in his religion. The New Testament story of Jesus and the little children has been used for centuries to teach a particular type of spiritual childhood. Pointing to a little child, Jesus said to his disciples, "Unless you change and become like little children, you will never enter the kingdom of heaven" (Mt 18:3). Jesus did not explain what qualities of the child he had in mind. The tendency has been to assume that Jesus was referring to the child's duty to obey his parents or to the child's willingness to believe whatever he is told. But is it not just as possible that Jesus was referring to the unending curiosity of children, or to the way they so readily adapt to changes, or to their continuous desire for new things? At any rate, St. Paul did not seem to think he was violating anything Jesus taught by making this statement about leaving childhood behind: "When I was a child, I spoke as a child, I felt as a child, I thought as a child. Now that I have become a man, I have put away the things of a child" (1Cor 13:11).

In studying religious development as it occurs in the lives of ordinary people, three aspects may be noted. The first aspect is the development of behaviors. Children *do* things before they understand them. A child can draw with crayons or splash watercolors without knowing anything about art; he enjoys doing things just for the sake of doing them. He does not need a reason for doing things, and he does not expect any particular outcomes. He simply likes to play. The small child especially likes to play at imitating grown-ups. He likes grown-ups to teach him to do things. Thus parents find it easy to teach a child some religious behavior, such as praying, and the child will do it regularly without necessarily understanding it.

The second aspect is the development of understanding. Although understanding may come before behavior for an adult, for children behavior precedes understanding. First children do something, then they begin to understand it. Nearly everybody begins his religious education as a small child and so learns behaviors before understanding them. Children go to church, fold their hands, and say prayer words a long time before they grasp what it is all about. There is some truth in the quip about the child who told his mother that in Sunday school all the children had learned to sing "Gladys, the Cross-eyed Bear" ("Gladly, the Cross I'd Bear"). Small children can take pleasure and satisfy needs just from doing rituals. The need for understanding represents a later stage in development.

The third aspect of development is experience. It is one

thing to go to church, another to understand why, and still another to experience it as something that touches the delicate part of you and changes you. Experience is both the beginning and the goal of development. A child's first experience of the world is religious. To a small child the world is a mysterious place filled with awe and guided by some sort of personality. Only later does a child develop a concept of nature and of a world ruled by laws of nature. Although the way a person experiences the world undergoes many changes, some sort of direct experience continues to be critical for development.

If it is a danger that people may remain bogged down in behaviors without any understanding of why they do them, it is an even greater danger that people may become so involved in searching for understanding that they never experience anything. We live in a mind-centered culture. Schools, which are supposed to prepare a person for life, concentrate almost exclusively on knowledge. Fortunately, society makes room for artists too—painters, musicians, actors, poets, and novelists—who try to give us experiences. Although some sort of knowledge, perhaps a vague knowledge, may be necessary to have an experience, the experience is more than knowledge. Man finds fulfillment not in knowing about science but in experiencing scientific discovery, not in knowing about art but in experiencing music or a painting, not in knowing about food but in experiencing a good meal, not in knowing about religion but in experiencing it.

Several scientific studies of religious development have been made. In the pages that follow, the results of these studies will be used to trace religious development, beginning with the religion of a small child and ending with the religion of a middle-aged person. No attempt will be made to describe the religion of an elderly person. Although the elderly seem to have attained a simple and wise view of religion, not much information has been accumulated about religious development in later life. Neither will any effort be made to describe perfectly mature religious development. Rather, the effort will be to describe how religion is viewed and practiced and fitted into the personality structure of typical people.

Thought and Discussion: (1) Does the concept of specialization apply to religion? Is it necessary for laymen to depend on clergymen to define religious behavior and to provide religious understanding and experiences? (2) Do you think that most adults are religiously mature? What do you base your impression on? (3) Does each person tend to emphasize just one aspect of religion—either behaviors, or understanding, or experiences? Which aspect do you emphasize? (4) Is it enough for a person to have deep experiences even if he has very little intellectual understanding of religion?

The Religion of a Five-Year-Old

Johnny is five years old. His parents are church-going Christians, not overly pious people but people who have found some value in their religion and who want to transmit it to their children. Johnny has a sister a few years older than himself. On Sunday the whole family goes to church together. The massive church fascinates Johnny. It has lights hanging by long chains from the ceiling which seem to be waiting for Tarzan to leap out and swing from one to the next, all the way down the church and out the big front door. When Johnny turns around to imagine this or to check on the baby gurgling merrily a few pews back, his sister pokes him on the shoulder and gestures that he should face up front. As he does, mother gives him a neat little smile. The stained glass windows are pretty when the sun is hitting them directly. You can see how the colors are being reflected onto the pillars and onto the floor in the wide middle aisle. Some people have carved their initials into the benches. It was probably older boys, thinks Johnny, and they must have done it when their mothers and fathers were not with them.

Mother likes to sit up straight and watch the altar. Father always has his head bowed down; it is hard to tell if he is praying or if he is falling asleep. As for sister, she keeps on taking her handkerchief out of her pocketbook and then putting it back in, obviously tempting someone to grab it from her. Father is bound to look up the second you try it. It is singing time now, and everybody is singing the song written on the sheets. Some of these people sing worse than cats and dogs. The man up at the altar is not very interesting to watch. He does not do much. He talks a lot. Everybody hears him talking to God. God never talks back. But God comes down from heaven into the cup with the wine in it and into the little pieces of bread. People eat these and have God in them. You are a pretty good person if you have been to church.

There is a crucifix on the wall over Johnny's bed. He has been taught to look at it when he says his prayers each night. He will tell you that that is God on it, and he was nailed on it by the Jews. He died. He is in heaven now. He sees everything and knows everything you do. If you pray to him he will protect you when you are sleeping. You can also get things by praying for them. You should pray for everybody. First you should say the Our Father:

Our Father, wart in heaven,
hollowedbethy name . . .

Johnny has been taught that God made him. His parents have tried to give him a little bit of sex education. He knows he was not dropped at the front door by a stork. God started him growing in his mother's belly, and when he got big enough he came out. As a matter of fact, God made everything. He controls everything. If you lift up your hand, it is because God makes you lift it up. Since God makes everything, we have to thank him for whatever we have. That is why we say grace before meals and why we thank God for things when we say our prayers. If it were not for God, we would not have anything.

When it comes to right and wrong, Johnny feels that whatever his parents approve of is right and whatever they disapprove of is wrong. Children may be bad but all grownups are good—except, of course, murderers and thieves. All laws and rules are eternal and unchangeable. Parents teach them to their children because they learned them from their parents, who in turn learned them from their parents, and so on back to the time when God gave them to the first parents. Since all rules come ultimately from God, no rules can be changed.

It is always bad to break a rule, no matter what. If the rule is to say your prayers before you go to sleep and you fall asleep in the car on the way home from grandmother's without having said your prayers, that is a sin and God will punish you for it. The severity of the sin depends on how much damage you do. It is worse to break three dishes when you are trying to help your mother set the table than to break one dish by throwing it at your sister. The circumstances in each case do not make any difference. A person should always be punished if he does something bad, even if he is sorry and is not going to do it again. After God punishes you, he will forgive you.

Thought and Discussion: (5) What is good in Johnny's religious development at this stage? (6) Is it possible for a five-year-old to be more mature than the one described above? (7) What are some of the ideas that Johnny should outgrow as he matures? (8) Should Johnny be brought to church on Sunday? (9) Should Johnny's parents try to teach him anything about religion?

The Religion of a Ten-Year-Old

Jane is ten years old. She is a Catholic and has been going to religion class for four years. When she goes to church with her family on Sunday she has some understandings of what the Mass is all about. Two ideas of the Mass stand out in her mind. One is that it is a sacrifice in which all things, especially Jesus, are offered to God so that he will forgive sins and grant his blessings. The other idea she has of the Mass is that it is a meal in which everybody is invited to eat the body and blood of Jesus and that eating this meal unites all who do. Most of the words of the Mass are understandable to her. She likes to sing when people around her are singing but not when she seems to be the only one. Going to Mass on Sunday is an obligation, she believes, but it is not a sin to miss for a very good reason.

Apart from the Mass, Jane's prayers are private. She usually says a few prayers before retiring at night, although sometimes she skips them. She prefers to pray in her own words rather than say specific prayer formulas over and over again. When she needs something very badly or is troubled by fearful thoughts or upset by a difficult situation, she prays very intently. In her room she keeps a crucifix, and sometimes she wears a medal.

Jane realizes that her prayers are not always answered.

Some of her most intense prayers concerning very important things in her life have gone unanswered. Doubts sometimes discourage her from praying. More often, she prays anyway. She believes that if a prayer is not answered it is because God knows what is best for us. When we get to heaven we will understand why some of our prayers were not answered.

On one hand, she believes that God is controlling everything that happens in the world and that he will make it all work out favorably in the end. On the other hand, she believes in laws of nature. The laws of nature, however, are under God's control. He can stop them or change them at any time. This is what happens in the case of miracles.

Jane is only beginning to become aware of some apparent contradictions in her thinking. It is hard for her to reconcile the idea that God is good with the idea of hell, or the idea that God is a loving father with the idea that he is pleased by the sacrifice of his Son, or the idea that he is concerned about us with the fact that he does not answer some very important prayers. The doubts raised in her mind by these apparent contradictions do not stay long or deeply upset her. She is persuaded that somehow these things must make sense but that she is incapable of understanding them.

The Bible has become an important part of Jane's religion. She is familiar with many Old Testament stories as well as many New Testament incidents about Jesus, his miracles, and his preaching to the people. She believes that everything in the Bible happened exactly as described, even though her teachers seem to suggest that some of the Old Testament stories are not one-hundred-percent accurate. From the Bible she got the idea that God used to speak directly to people in ancient times and that he gave prophets knowledge of the future. Since God does not speak to us anymore, Jane thinks of God as a figure from ancient history.

The New Testament stories make Jesus very real for her. In her mind Jesus and God are the same thing. She has a very deep love and admiration for Jesus. She prays to him.

Jane tends to be a bit of a pharisee. In her the family has a religious watchdog. She lets people know how she feels about an aunt who does not go to church. If mother does some housework or father sets out to fix something on Sunday, they are likely to be reminded that Sunday is supposed to be a day of rest. Jane has a particular interest in the behavior of her brothers and sisters. She lets them know when they are doing wrong. She also has some definite feelings about being a Catholic. Although she does not know much about Protestants or Jews, she is sure that it is better to be a Catholic. These other religions are false in her mind. She tries to be big about it and admits that these other people *think* that they are practicing true religions.

Thought and Discussion: (10) In what ways is Jane more mature than a five-year-old? In what ways is Jane still religiously immature? (11) Is Jane a typical ten-year-old? (12) Has Jane reached a mature understanding of prayer? (13) Is Jane's way of thinking about God mature? (14) Is Jane right in feeling that she should accept beliefs even though she cannot understand them? (15) How should one react to the ten-year-old's strong identification with a particular religious group?

The Religion of a Fifteen-Year-Old

Bob is a member of a Protestant church. His family goes to church rather frequently and often participates in church events. Bob himself belongs to a youth group in the church which holds discussions, does projects in the community now and then, and which also provides a number of recreational activities. Quite a few of Bob's friends belong to the group too. For them the youth group is the kernel of what the church has to offer, for this is where they most strongly experience Christian fellowship with one another. The group is also the vehicle in which they enter the organization of the church. The group is sometimes given a role in the Sunday worship and in other church events, is also an opportunity to act as a helping hand of the church reaching into the neighborhood to perform special projects for the community. If it were not for the youth group, Bob probably would not have much involvement in the church.

Bob has some trouble matching his idea of himself to his idea of a religious person. He realizes that he is not perfect in his behavior towards others and that he depends on God for his very existence. But he cannot think of himself as a Charlie Brown doomed to continual failure and helplessness despite his best intentions. He believes that people are basically good and that a person should not spend too much time thinking about how he is a sinner. He is aware that some of the other teenagers in the group seem to have had moving religious experiences of a sort he has not had. They speak of God and Jesus with more deep feeling than he could express. For some of them prayer seems to be a kind of mystical experience, something which is rare for him.

Bob's idea of sin has matured quite a bit. He believes that a person has to be guided by his own conscience. A person's intentions are important in judging whether he did right or wrong. There is still a lot of revenge in Bob's moral thinking. He thinks a person ought to be punished when he has done wrong, even if he has repented and the punishment can do no further good. Bob—and his parents— think he is mature enough to know what is right and wrong.

Bob accepts God as a sort of helper when he is down or when he wants something. Sometimes he prays before falling asleep at night. Most often he is too tired or he forgets. Every now and then he tries to make up for it by praying a little more than usual. He spends a lot of time daydreaming about himself and about what he wants to do with his life. Maybe this is another way of praying, but he does not recognize it as such. He does not connect religion with his home life or his plans for the future. Religion is something separate, sealed off in a different part of his mind from these other things.

Many doubts about what he was taught have upset Bob's beliefs. Much of the Bible, particularly Old Testament stories like the one about Adam and Eve, he no longer believes. He has outgrown a childish attitude toward the Bible which accepts everything in it as strict history. Teachers have told him that Bible writers exaggerated or even made up some of these stories. Yet his understanding of the Bible is not very developed. He has swung from the belief that it is all true to the belief that none of it is true without really studying the Bible.

Because Bob has a growing mind and a developing body he has more doubts and many new interests, especially sex. He knows that he is no longer a child, but he knows he is not yet an adult either. In many situations he does not know how he should behave. There is also the fact that he is more independent now and occasionally has disagreements with his parents. All these things give him the feeling that he is not as good a person as he was four or five years ago. But he really wants to be a good person.

Thought and Discussion: (16) Is Bob as good a person as five-year-old Johnny or ten-year-old Jane? (17) What features of the religion of childhood would you expect a fifteen-year-old to be outgrowing? (18) In what ways does Bob still have to mature religiously? (19) Some churches emphasize the experience of a religious "conversion" during adolescence. Is such an experience necessary for religious development?

The Religion of a Young Adult

Frank is twenty-two. He graduated from college several months ago and is living at home while working for a downtown business concern. On Sundays he goes to church with his girlfriend. Just a few years back going to church seemed a very boring and unimportant thing to him. For a while he did not go. But after he had been dating Sharon a while, he started going to church with her. Sometimes going to church is a very deep experience for him. At other times, it is more a matter of routine. Although he believes that people should practice their religion, he does not think that religious practices are as important as trying to be a good person day by day.

Now and then Frank prays, even though he is not sure that God answers prayers. He is not really certain about most of his religion. In high school he had begun questioning his beliefs more and more until he was challenging everything during his freshman year in college. Next to dating, religion was the biggest topic in bull sessions with his college friends. His thinking became much more liberal. For a time he could see no good in any of the organized churches, but he grew more firm in his belief in God and more aware of the Jesus of history. Jesus struck him as a truly religious man, a great spiritual leader, and a revolutionary reformer. Apart from belief in God and commitment to what Jesus stood for, various other religious beliefs and practices seem somewhat secondary to Frank. He may have his doubts about some of them, but they do not seem worth spending a lot of time thinking over. He is content now to be a church-going Christian without necessarily agreeing with everything he was taught as a child.

Frank believes in a personal God who is somehow concerned about human affairs. Whether God ever steps into history or just watches human affairs from the outside is a question Frank has not answered for himself. Neither is he sure that God will condemn or reward people in an afterlife, although he is inclined to think that there will be some sort of judgment. To Frank, God is the creator, and this is enough reason for prayer, worship, and living a good life.

As far as Frank is concerned, religion is something bigger than going to church, saying prayers, believing certain things, or even living a good life. Religion is something that helps a person find meaning for his life. Unlike the ant that goes about its daily work without any memory of its past or any notion of its future or any question about why it is digging tunnels in the ground, a human being wants to know why he exists. Religion helps Frank form some idea of what life is all about.

Frank does not talk much about his religion. He realizes that many of his friends think of religion as something unnecessary, if not harmful. What Frank finds in religion they look for in their careers and in their families. For them it is enough to be aware of social problems and to be aware of their own attitudes towards life, work, their family, and the society in which they live. They do not think any less of Frank for his religion, but they find it unnecessary for themselves. Consequently, Frank's religion is more private now than it had been a few years earlier when religion was more a part of his relationships and discussions with others.

Thought and Discussion: (20) In what ways is the religion of the young adult different from the religion of a teenager? (21) Are there any ways in which Frank is less mature religiously than the fifteen-year-old? (22) What has the young adult done with the doubts he had about his religion when he was a teenager?

The Religion of a Middle-aged Person

Mrs. Green is the wife of a service station owner and the mother of three children. She is a Catholic and goes to church every Sunday with her husband and children. Apart from momentary distractions, noticing what people are wearing and which young people are going together, she is quite attentive to the Mass, saying the prayers, singing, and watching the priest. The Mass means a lot to her. Her knowledge of it is no greater than her children's, but she senses more deeply the ideas of sacrifice and thanksgiving expressed in the Mass because she has had more experience of what it means to sacrifice herself.

The experiences of living—disappointments, illnesses, bereavements, births, weddings, and raising children—have all affected Mrs. Green's religious outlook. Religion has been a part of the happiest as well as the saddest moments of her life. She recalls the priest who said her wedding Mass and baptized her children and buried her father. Since religion is associated with so many important events in her life, Mrs. Green will probably always be a sincere member of the church. Whatever shortcomings she may find in the church are outweighed by the values and cherished moments it has given her.

Mrs. Green prays a little more frequently than she did before she was married, but there is not much difference in the way she prays. She has faith that prayers are answered by God if it is good for the person praying. Somehow God is in control of the universe, she believes, and although we cannot understand why things happen as they do, all things happen according to God's plan. Everything will work out for the best in the end. In general, her beliefs adhere very closely to the preaching she hears in church on Sunday and to what she was taught as a little girl. She regards the priest as a spokesman for God.

Of late, however, some bewilderment has challenged Mrs. Green's long-established beliefs. The parish priests do not seem to be in complete agreement with each other. It is well known among the women in the parish that certain ones condemn birth control pills while others say they are all right. They do not seem to have the same beliefs about other things either, such as whether there is a hell and whether the Catholic church is the only true one. The young priests seem to be different from the old ones. When changes in the Mass and in Lenten regulations were first introduced, Mrs. Green was upset because she had been taught that these things could not be changed. Eventually she accepted the changes and came to favor them over the old ways. But the differences in beliefs that seem so common nowadays, particularly when seen among priests, tax her understanding. She wonders whether the church is being modernized too much and too fast. Nobody seems to know what to believe or what rules of conscience to follow.

What especially troubles Mrs. Green is the religion her children are being taught. Two go to Catholic schools and one goes to C.C.D. classes. Their religion books are nothing like the Baltimore Catechism she learned in school as a young girl. They are bigger, more full of opinions it seems, and, it must be admitted, a bit more attractive with their pictures. The religion books seem to say a great deal about loving your neighbor but not so much about God and the church. Most of the religion classes seem to be spent on topics like racism, poverty, personality, war.

What is more, Mrs. Green disagrees with some of the opinions expressed by her children's religion teachers on these topics. She expects her children to be different from herself in their knowledge of other subjects, like the new math or social studies. Religion, however, is a subject in which she expects her children to have the same ideas as she has. The new religion seems to be another thing separating her from her children. She wants religion to do the opposite, to create more agreement and similarity between herself and her children.

The difficulty Mrs. Green has understanding why her children's religion classes often focus on social issues is partly due to her idea that religion is a separate aspect of life which has nothing to do with business, changes in society, or politics, except, of course, when it comes to condemning communism. As far as she understands, religion is concerned with God, with going to church and saying prayers, and with keeping the commandments. She was taught to believe in separation of church and state, with a resulting separation of religion from social and political issues.

Thought and Discussion: (23) In what ways is Mrs. Green religiously mature? In what ways is she not? (24) Is her attitude toward the church reasonable? her attitude toward priests? (25) Why do changes in the church upset her? (26) Should Mrs. Green be so concerned with her children's religious beliefs? (27) How can she prevent a religious generation gap from developing between herself and her children?

Summary

On the basis of several studies that have been made, we have described the religious outlooks of persons of various ages from early childhood to middle age. Although individuals differ greatly from one another, certain general trends are visible in religious development. Beliefs which are accepted from parents and teachers during childhood tend to be questioned during adolescence and then either rejected or accepted in the light of new understandings. Moral attitudes, which are very rigid in childhood, become more flexible after the questioning of adolescence, and personal conscience becomes more important than rules laid down by authorities. Prayer and church attendance, which are largely mechanical actions in early childhood, remain as part of the teenager's religion only to the extent that he can find new forms of prayer and church services that are particularly suited to his own needs. It is especially in late adolescence that religion becomes a great personal concern and even a common topic of conversation with friends. The majority of adults have decided either to accept or to reject most of the beliefs and practices taught them in childhood. They seem to have settled the matter of religion for themselves. They have turned their attention from themselves to the religious development of their children.

IN GOD WE TRUST

1964

Anna Maria

Chapter 2

Why People Are Religious

In the last chapter we described the religious feelings, attitudes, beliefs, and behaviors of persons at different stages in life from childhood to middle age. It is relatively easy to conduct surveys which give us such descriptions. These descriptions, however, are like snapshots of a person taken at various ages. We are left wondering what processes caused the person to develop from one stage to the next. That is the question we turn to now. In this chapter we will look at processes by which a person's religious sentiments develop through the years. Because some of the same processes that explain religious development also explain rejection of religion, a discussion of religious rejection will also be included.

Here it is important to become aware of the limits of what can be said of religious development. People are so different from one another that a discussion of personal religion, or any other aspect of personality, is bound to be limited to generalities which, while they convey some truth about a large number of people, seldom are the whole truth for a given individual. The processes to be described do not apply equally to all individuals and only more or less to a particular person. Although we can say with confidence that a person's religion has been influenced by the culture in which he lives, by his religious training or lack of it, by his personal needs, and by his life experiences, it is impossible to specify exactly how much each of these has contributed to his present religious outlook.

If it is impossible to make such an accounting looking back over a person's life, it is equally impossible to make any predictions for the future or to plan any sure-fire program of religious development. Formulas for religious development have to be expressed in terms of probabilities, not certainties. The individual is more complex than we could specify, and his freedom encompasses more possibilities than anyone could control or even list.

Cultural Influences

A very effective, though indefinable, process through which religion becomes part of one's personality is *acculturation*, that is, the process whereby a person absorbs qualities from the culture in which he lives. Each society has its own culture, including a particular way of looking at the world and a particular style of living. Thus an American tends to see the world as a bundle of opportunities he can take advantage of; for this reason he develops a style of living based on continuous striving to get more of what the society has to offer. Nobody gives lessons in living this way, yet we absorb them from the culture. From birth we are immersed in a culture from which we learn not only patterns of behavior but also a particular style of thinking and feeling.

Usually by culture we mean the traditions and lifestyle of a particular nation (or of a group of nations clustered together). Still, within cultures we can recognize subcultures, by which we mean groups of people who are different in some ways from other groups in the same culture. Within each national culture there are usually male and female subcultures; lower-, middle-, and upper-class subcultures; child, youth, and adult subcultures; urban and rural subcultures; and any number of others. We have as many subcultures as we have groups of people with distinct styles of living. Men and women are not expected to have the same interests or behave in the same way; neither are children and adults, city-dwellers and farmers, tycoons and laborers. Each of these groups has a subculture of its own.

How much of a place does religion have in various cultures and subcultures? Since 1940 Gallup Polls have tried to answer this question. Faced with the difficult problem of measuring the amount of religion different groups of people have, the polls have used church attendance as a standard. Admittedly, going to church may not be the most valid indication that a person is religious, but it is the best that has been used so far.

Of the eleven countries surveyed in the 1968 Gallup Poll (*New York Times*, December 21, 1968), the one with the greatest church attendance was the United States, where 43 percent of the population attended church in a given week. The rate of church attendance in the United States was even higher than the rate in such traditionally religious countries as Spain. In West Germany, France, and Uruguay the rate of church attendance was around 25 percent, and in the Scandinavian countries it was lowest, with only about 5 percent of the population in Finland going to church.

The Gallup Poll conducted at the end of 1971 (*New York Times*, January 9, 1972) restricted itself to church attendance within the United States. It showed that attendance has continued to decline slowly, as it has been doing since 1958, although more people attend church now than in 1940. According to religious groups, Catholics are the most church-going (57 percent), Protestants next (37 percent), and Jews last (19 percent). However, attendance rates have been declining most rapidly among Catholics, of whom 71 percent attended church in the peak year of 1964.

Among other subcultures within the United States, women have been more church-going than men (45 percent compared to 35 percent), and non-whites have been more church-going than whites (44 percent compared to 40 percent). These surveys have not included persons under 21. The lowest rate of church attendance has always been among persons 21-29 years old (28 percent in 1971), with higher rates and less difference between those 40-49 years old (42 percent in 1971) and those 50 and over (45 percent in 1971). There has been slightly more church attendance in large communities than in small ones.

Social class structures also seem to affect religious practice but in different ways over the years. In 1968 people with higher education levels and higher incomes were the most church-going. Forty-one percent of persons with only a grade school education went to church in a given week, compared to 47 percent of those with a college education. Forty percent of those from families with an income of less than $3,000 a year attended church regularly, while 45 percent of those from families with an income of more than $7,000 went to church. It seemed that a person became more religious as he moved up the social ladder. The churches seemed to be appealing more to the middle class than to the poor. But the 1971 survey showed that church-going dropped considerably among the more educated (from 47 percent down to 40 percent), while it has remained the same among the less educated (at 41 percent). The churches seem to be losing their attractiveness to persons with higher education.

Despite differences among subcultures, American society seems to be one of the most religious in the Western world. The strength of religion in American culture is evident in many ways: in the affluence of churches and in their financial and political influence; in the various publicity given religious themes by all the general media and in the public tributes to God displayed on coins and buildings. With religion so thoroughly permeating the culture, even if an American is not religious himself, he is likely to be at least tolerant of religion. To be actively anti-religious, or just to be personally atheistic, goes against the culture and incurs the disapproval of other Americans.

One process, then, that explains why people are religious is acculturation. We absorb religion from the culture of our society. Acculturation is not so intensive as formal religious training, but it is far more extensive. A person may be subjected to religious training in specific situations for a few years of his life; acculturation continues over a whole lifetime and takes place everywhere a person goes as long as he remains in the society.

Still, acculturation does not explain entirely why a person is religious. There are people in the same society equally exposed to the same process of acculturation who are not religious. Though culture can favor or disfavor religion, there are still other influences at work in the individual.

Thought and Discussion: (1) It seems easier and more rewarding to be religious than to be non-religious in America. Is this the reason why many Americans are religious? (2) Why is church attendance much higher in the U.S. than in other countries? (3) Why has church-going dropped so much among more highly educated persons? (4) How does the religion of the teenage subculture (about ages 13-17) and of

the youth subculture (about ages 18-22) compare with the
overall American pattern?

Personal Needs

The culture is something outside of us which influences
our behavior and which we in turn may influence by our
behavior. In addition to the culture surrounding us, however, there are processes operating from within us that help
to explain our behavior. We are aware that something within us may move us to action when nothing in the environ-
ment seems to be beckoning, like a person who feels an urge
for a cup of coffee in the morning even before the perking
pot releases its aroma, or the person who feels he must dress
formally when no one is demanding it of him.

For the present, let us call these internal processes which
move us to action "needs." This implies that we are incomplete, growing beings who can find fulfillment only by reaching beyond what we already have within us. We are always
reaching out and immersing ourselves in the world around
us because it is only through an exchange with the rest of
creation that we can fulfill ourselves. Though the thin layer
of skin surrounding our bodies seems to separate us from
the rest of the world, it is really a living membrane ushering
through itself a continuous stream of chemicals and impressions that bind the within-us to the without-us.

Our needs are not entirely innate. Human beings have
no inborn patterns of behavior determined by heredity
alone. Although behavior patterns are rooted in innate
abilities, some element of learning goes into the development of every style of thinking and behaving and feeling.
The learning may take place by way of vague processes
like acculturation or by way of very specific training, as in

learning to write one's name. Such basic needs as eating and sleeping are influenced by learning too, so that a person going from one culture to another must learn to digest different foods, to eat at different times, and to sleep at different times and under different conditions.

Needs also differ from one age to another. Some needs absent at birth emerge later in life, like sex and the need for meaning in life. Other needs vary in intensity from one age to another; perhaps the need for security will predominate in childhood, the need for new experiences in adolescence, the need for meaning in youth, the need for accomplishment in middle age. People's needs are ever-changing.

Since the peculiar circumstances of each individual's life influence the development of his needs, needs also tend to be personal. Not everyone feels equally the need for security or the need for privacy or the need for intimacy. Still, human beings everywhere seem to have, more or less, a certain common stock of needs which, despite the cultural variations in which they are dressed, point to some underlying innate human strivings. There is a shared hereditary humanity that makes human beings more like than unlike each other.

All this background about needs will help us fill in another part of the reason why people are religious. An enormous list of needs could be drawn up and discussed from the viewpoint of the way they may affect religious development, but for the present a discussion of *three* needs will be sufficient. We will see how religious development may be influenced by the needs for *security*, *meaning*, and *closure* (which will be explained presently). For the sake of illustration, we will describe how each of these three needs operates within a certain group of people. For our example, we will use a "human relations laboratory."

A human relations laboratory is a group of people, usually strangers to one another, who have arranged to meet under the direction of a psychologist for the sake of giving each an opportunity to explore questions about how he relates to other people. Such meetings are often held on some old estate in the country.

When the participant arrives for the first meeting, he finds himself in a strange place with a dozen other people who are all strangers to each other. Nobody knows what is going to happen or what he is expected to do. Everyone suspects that some deep psychological probing is going to take place and that he is going to be exposed in front of these other people.

Nervousness pulsates from each person as the group assembles, entering one by one, in the large drawing room of the mansion. As they sit in the old chairs or stand by the windows flipping through magazines they are not reading, as they shoot quick glances at one another, from the dark clouds of their anxiety arises a vision. In their imaginations they begin to see the psychologist they are all waiting for. He knows everything about how people behave, he is understanding and sympathetic, and he will have complete control over this group. He will protect the weak personalities from the strong ones, he will allow no one to be hurt, he will ask nothing beyond one's strength, and he will allow only what is good for each person.

These fantasies the group develops about the psychologist are very much like mankind's fantasies about God. They are fantasies, not in the sense of being unreal necessarily, but in the sense of originating from within us rather than from the person in question. In particular, our need for *security* prompts us to believe, when we are in threatening situations, that we will be protected. Almost invariably the condemned criminal unto the very end experiences "the delusion of reprieve"; he cannot believe that he is really going to be executed. When death itself has actually struck, the living cling to the belief that the death is unreal and that the dead person is alive and well somewhere else.

We find ourselves on this earth like the strangers in the old mansion, uncertain of what is going to happen and of what will be expected of us. But we believe that we have a protector who is certain of our uncertainties, who controls what we cannot, and who will allow nothing ultimately to destroy us. This belief is rooted in our inner need for *security*. Though the seed of such a belief may have been the religious teachings of a church, it would not survive in us if it did not have the soil of an inner need in which to take root.

Another need affecting religious development is the need for *meaning*. Although a human relations laboratory is nothing more than people in a room observing how they act toward one another, participants start looking for deep meanings in the simplest things. If there happens to be one chair too few, they conjecture that the psychologist planned it that way to see what the reaction would be to one person not having a seat. The layout of the chairs, the lighting of the room, a key in the lock of the door, a mirror on the wall—all these circumstances are thought to have been deliberately arranged by the psychologist for some special purpose, although, in fact, he may not have even noticed some of these circumstances. One person wants to light up a cigarette, another wants to look at his watch and see what time it is, the lady in the corner wants to clear her throat, but none of them do it because they think the psychologist will see some deep meaning in it. In short, everything about the place and everything one does is imagined to have some meaning beyond the obvious, and the psychologist is the person who is thought to know these meanings.

It is much the same with religious attitudes toward the world and human behavior. Everything in the world is thought to be purposely arranged by God and all human behavior is thought to have a dimension more meaningful in the eyes of God than we can perceive. The concept of chance is not seriously considered as an explanation for how the world is. Human behavior takes on an eternal significance because of divine merit attached to it or because it fits into a divine plan. This tendency to look for purpose and meaning beyond the face value of things is an essential part of the religious attitude toward the world. Religion is one of the ways in which our need for meaning may seek fulfillment.

Religion as a personal trait is also affected by our need for *closure*, i.e., our need for having things completed, not left hanging. The people in a human relations laboratory expect the psychologist in the final meeting to explain what underlying forces have been influencing the group's behavior and to sum up what has been accomplished. On a more everyday level, we expect a movie to have a definite ending, naturally with the good guys winning and the bad guys losing; we are inclined to rearrange a single flower which is jutting way out on one side of a bouquet; we want to straighten a picture on the wall if it is not lined up with the horizontals of the ceiling and the floor. We like a finished design.

In religion, too, this need for symmetry and completion finds expression, but on a much grander scale. Religion tends to impose an order and a final completion on the world. God is supposed to be like the tapestry maker who is working out a beautiful pattern although we from the other side may see only a jumbled web of multi-colored threads. In the end, we will see the pattern God is working out. He will sum up for us what we have done in the world. The irregularities will be straightened; specifically, the bad will be punished and the good rewarded. God is planning a neat conclusion to everything. Our need for closure helps us to believe this.

We could list other needs and show how they may operate in religion. The point is, however, that religion itself is not a specific need or an instinct. It is a blanketing trait that stretches over many needs, a trait that sinks roots into many different needs and that offers some degree of fulfillment to these diverse needs. It is true that these needs vary in intensity from one person to the next and that they differ somewhat from one culture to another, so that the religion of one person or of one culture is likely to be different from the religion of others.

Thought and Discussion: (5) Would you agree that the religion of a child is based primarily on a need for security? On what needs would the religion of a teenager be based? The religion of an adult? (6) Which needs most strongly influence your own religious outlook? (7) Since needs vary from one culture to another, isn't it better to have a variety of religious styles rather than just one? (8) Since needs vary from one age in life to another, should parents expect their teenage children to have the same religious outlook as themselves? (9) St. Augustine said that when he traveled from one city to another studying philosophy in search of God, it was a futile effort because all the time God was present in himself. In what sense is God in human nature?

Religious Training and Experiences

Many people receive direct religious training, which in early childhood is an intensified indoctrination into the religious style of the family, probably religious schooling in the practices and beliefs of the local church during later childhood and adolescence, and perhaps, what is becoming much more common nowadays, adult religious education. How much religious development can be credited to such training or instruction?

Although extensive research has been carried out to assess the effects of Lutheran and Catholic religious schools on their students, the research has not been sufficiently probing or sensitive to yield hard and fast conclusions. Yet some general statements are suggested by the data. It seems that as far as their religion goes, the teenagers in religious high schools do not differ in any appreciable way from teenagers in public schools. Those in religious schools show a slightly more advanced religious vocabulary in tune with present-day religious instruction, but this more sophisticated vocabulary does not carry with it any deeper understanding of religious beliefs. The beliefs, and an understanding of them, of students in religious schools and of those in public schools are virtually the same. Likewise, there is no evidence to indicate that there is any difference between parochial school students and public school students in their religious practices, either private practices, such as prayer, or public practices, such as church attendance. One study indicated that the majority of Catholic high school students feel that their religion classes have had *no* effect on them. While about 18 percent feel that religion classes have had some good effects on them, about 17 percent feel that religion classes have had some bad effects on them. Nevertheless, the vast majority of Catholic high school students favor retaining some religious instruction in their school curriculum.

The difficulty of eliciting the thoughts and feelings of grade school children seems to have discouraged extensive research, and so we are left with a large question mark over the effects of religious training in childhood. But the available evidence suggests that the real differentiating factor between individuals who are rather religious and those who are less religious is the person's family background. In other words, the religious climate of the family, which exercises its effect before the child goes to school, is the determining factor in religious development. Religious schools only enhance family effects.

No one would maintain that the family is the sole factor or that religious development is complete before the child is old enough to go to school. What is engendered in early childhood is a general attitude toward religion that may be a receptive attitude or a rejecting attitude. All later experiences touching the person encounter this attitude and either strengthen it—the more likely tendency—or weaken it. The basic attitude is always very difficult to change. It has a gravitational power that pulls incoming experiences into orbit around it.

Rather than change a basic attitude, a person is more likely to ignore or rationalize an experience. For example, if a person believes that God answers prayers and a prayer of his is not heard, instead of changing his belief he will probably look for some defect in the way he prayed or look for some reason why God should not have answered his prayer. On the other hand, if a person does not believe in praying and yet is driven to pray in some dire circumstances and the prayer is apparently answered, he will probably say, when the difficulty is over, that it was just a lucky coincidence. A person's basic attitude suggests the interpretations of events.

Studies of how wartime experiences affected the religious sentiments of veterans have shown that whether an experience deepened or weakened the religious beliefs of a soldier depended, not on the event, but on the disposition of the soldier. The same event would quicken one man's religious beliefs and shatter another's, according to the firmness of the person's prior convictions.

Granting that religious training has its greatest effects in early childhood when the basic attitude is established, what processes are involved? Religious training, like other kinds of learning, involves at least three processes: *identification*, *association*, and *conditioned responses*. Although most potent in childhood, these processes operate all through life.

Identification is a sort of imitation. The child imitates his parents and is usually rewarded, at least with affection, for doing so. In later childhood there is a period of particularly intensive hero worship during which the child models himself after greatly admired persons from real life or from fictions like the movies. Younger teenagers tend to imitate older ones. Although imitation continues through later life, it becomes increasingly more selective, more subtle, and more focused on real persons with whom one has contact. High school and college students may particularly imitate well-liked teachers. Middle-aged people may adopt mannerisms or sentiments from friends or business associates.

The concept of identification implies more than imitation, however. Imitation suggests something external and visible. Identification means absorbing the internal qualities of another person, actually grasping his feelings and convictions and making them part of oneself. The difference is sometimes glaring. The child who sees his parents go to church and participate in church activities, not out of religious conviction so much as social convention, will probably identify rather than imitate. That is, he will adopt the religious sentiments of his parents rather than their religious practice. The opposite case may also occur. A child with parents of genuine religious outlook but with few religious practices will probably adopt the religious mentality of his parents and, in an effort to achieve inner consistency, may take on more religious practices than they. Even very young children can penetrate the masks of their elders and grasp their true inner sentiments.

A second learning process involved in religious development is *association*. In our minds things may become associated with one another or with certain feelings from having been experienced together in the past. A fork is usually associated with a knife, balloons with carnivals and parties, rain with gloom. On the religious side, a church may be associated with childhood, a clergyman with one's wedding, religious holidays with new clothes and family banquets, the Bible with Sunday school lessons, church services with boring sermons.

A person's associations depend on his experiences. When the clergy keep pressing parishioners for more contributions, religion becomes associated with money grubbing. When a mother continually pesters her children about religious practices, religion becomes associated with a nagging mother. When religion is used to threaten a child with punishment from God for being bad, religion becomes associated with oppressive intimidation. When a teenager joins a church youth group doing neighborhood work, religion becomes associated with social involvement. When the clergy go out to meet and help their parishioners, religion becomes associated with being friendly and concerned for others. Depending on whether they are favorable or not, associations draw us toward or repel us from religion.

Besides identification and association, religious training involves *conditioned responses*; this simply means that a person is conditioned, or trained, to make a certain response in a certain situation. Most Christians, for example, are conditioned in early childhood to have particular feelings of reverence, of seriousness, of mystery, of being in the presence of God when they are in a church. A child may be conditioned to have feelings of sorrow for sin whenever he sees a crucifix. Another person may be conditioned to be unquestioning and submissive in the presence of a priest.

Conditioning is the result of direct training at an impressionable time. Once accomplished, it is extremely difficult to undo. The person who has consciously turned away from the religion in which he was brought up may very well continue to feel the conditioned responses. A process that exercises such power over the personality can be validly used in education, including religious education, but great care should be taken in choosing what kinds of responses to condition. Most of us have been conditioned to some helpful and to some unhelpful responses.

Thought and Discussion: (10) Are religious schools worth maintaining? Why do so many parents send their children to religious schools? (11) What effects could one expect from adult religious education? (12) Since the most important religious training occurs in early childhood when the parents are the child's teachers, some people say that the churches should concentrate not on schools for the children but on adult education. Do you agree? (13) What conditioned responses do you have to clergymen? To what extent are these responses helpful or unhelpful when you meet a clergyman?

Rejection of Religion

Some of the same processes that explain why one person is religious could also explain why another person is not.

A person could be acculturated to being non-religious if he is brought up in a non-religious society. Training and experiences could also be arranged to reinforce a non-religious outlook on life. If the religion, or part of it, seems to go contrary to needs, then needs could also explain a person's being non-religious. A religion that is highly directive, for example, might be rejected because it grates against a person's need to be self-directing.

Some periods of life generally seem to be more or less religious than others. The years from eight to twelve constitute what might be called "the good boy" stage of life when a child is very compliant; if the family is religious or if he goes to a religious school, the child will be faithfully religious. Of course, it is still the religion of a child. The teenage years and the youth years often seem less religious. Some research indicates that the mid- and late twenties are the least religious years of life. In the thirties there seems to be a religious renewal, and one often sees a profound religious spirit in old age. No doubt, these are gross generalities. Yet they suggest some speculations.

The apparent religious decline in adolescence requires more careful scrutiny than most alarmed parents undertake. Since the teenagers themselves usually think that they have been becoming progressively less religious, it is very easy to accept that judgment. There certainly does seem to be a decline in external religious behaviors, such as church attendance. Likewise certain religious beliefs easily accepted in childhood come to be questioned or rejected. Simultaneously, however, there is often an intensification of inner religious awareness and of religious feelings. In other words, what happens in adolescence may be not so much a religious decline—as if it would be easy to decline from the passively accepted religion of the good boy stage—as it is a sifting of beliefs and a shifting of emphasis from an external to an internal religion. This involves a movement toward acquiring a more personal religion which, while it embraces less than the religion of earlier years, embraces that smaller bit more firmly. The teenager has less religion, but what he has is more a part of him. Does that make him more or less religious?

Several explanations are commonly given for the fact that teenagers exhibit few external religious behaviors. One is that these behaviors are associated with childhood. Since the teenager is trying to get out of childhood in a hurry, religious practices may be left behind with dolls and toy dumptrucks. Sometimes adolescents also reject practices because they do not see them having any notable effects on many of the adults who perform them. Another explanation lies in the sexual awakening of adolescence, which is likely to be a factor when a particular religion takes a dim view of sex. And an explanation that should not be overlooked is that the religious rituals themselves may be overly monotonous or abstract.

A survey of several major American college campuses revealed that religion was a topic of conversation second only to sex. This suggests that the adolescent tendency toward greater religious awareness with more personal groping continues on into the youth years (roughly, the last part of high school and the college years). Perhaps the big difference is that the religion of adolescents tends not only to be inner but also to be private. In the youth years, religion is a shared experience as young people discuss their views with one another and search together for deeper understanding and for purposes in life. The private worlds of adolescents converge in the shared world of youths.

We can only speculate about what happens in the

twenties, when there seems to be a religious low. It may be that without the stimulation provided by something like a college atmosphere religious searching fades away, leaving the great questions of life unanswered in a satisfactory way. It may also be that, free from the family of childhood and not yet bound to a family of one's own, the young person enjoys a highly individualistic life style from which he eliminates whatever is not personally satisfying. A religion that has been practiced to please parents is quickly dropped when away from them.

Having children and settling down in a community may be the occasion for the increased religious orientation of the thirties. There are values in religion that parents want for their children, and in most communities religious affiliation is favorably regarded. The last religious shift, the tendency toward increased religious concern in old age, is often assumed to result from increasing awareness of death. Although there may be some truth in this explanation, it seems to slight the greater wisdom and the more profound outlook on life acquired through years of living. The searchings of adolescence and youth may not have paid off in theories and philosophical explanations, but they may be answered more directly and simply, and ever more fully, by the experience of life itself. The religion of old age, then, might be more intense, not because the old apparently have less time to live, but because they have already done more living.

Finally, a few words about what many people consider the ultimate religious decline, atheism. It is interesting to note that in societies that purposely set out to acculturate and condition atheism, the effort has been abandoned, though reluctantly, evidently because something in a person's needs seems to lean toward religion. Where the state has tried to give the people a comprehensive secular framework for living, such as Marxism, religion has survived and even revived. In Russian publications of late one may find scattered articles in favor of religion where once there were only articles opposing religion.

Still, there are people who regard themselves as atheists. Years ago religious writers simply dismissed them as immoral people. But there are no indications that atheists are any more or less moral than religious people. A person may find his needs fully satisfied by something other than religion, maybe by concern for his family or by dedication to his work or by involvement in social movements. Whether a person believes in God or not seems to make little difference in the way he lives if he can find meaning for his life in some way or other. Trends in contemporary theology might suggest that the atheist is religious anyway if he is concerned about loving his neighbor in whom God is invisibly present.

Thought and Discussion: (14) What should parents do if their teenager does not want to go to church? (15) Are the teenagers active in your church? Why, or why not? (16) Teenagers often regard the religion of adults as the same as the "good boy religion" of childhood. To what extent can the religion of people in their thirties be a mere regression to the religion of eight-year-olds? (17) Does being religious have any advantages over being an atheist (apart from theories about divine rewards and punishments)?

Summary

Although each person is a unique individual, there are some common factors that help to explain our religious development. For one thing, we share a common culture.

American culture puts a positive value on religion. Even if one does not personally regard himself as religious, our culture makes it difficult to take a negative attitude toward those who are. Another thing we all share is a common stock of basic human needs. Three needs which influence the development of a religious outlook are the needs for meaning in life, for security, and for closure. Other needs could be singled out, too, and their influence on religious development would become evident with some reflection. Religious training and experiences are a third common factor that most of us are affected by. It is in early childhood that religious training is most potent, but later experiences in life also make an impact. The child is more influenced by what his parents *are* than by what they do or say. Religion gradually acquires certain associations in the mind of a person, and religious training tends to implant conditioned religious responses. These same factors that help to explain how religion may become part of a personality also explain how other persons come to reject religion. A person's pattern of accepting or rejecting religion is affected by his culture, his needs, his training, and his experiences.

Chapter 3

Religion and Personality

Now that we have explored various stages of religious development, and the processes involved, we can ask how religion affects personality. Needless to say, a person's religion is part of his personality, so the question really should be stated: How does being religious affect the rest of one's personality? Before answering this question we will discuss briefly the relationship between psychology and religion.

Psychology and Religion

Psychology is concerned with the study of behavior. Although various branches of psychology study behaviors ranging from the reflexes of oysters to the dynamics of human mobs, most of us think of psychology as concerned with mental illness in human beings. Indeed, this is the concern of most psychologists, even of many who work all their lives in a lab with insects, pigeons, or something similar. The psychologist, like other scientists, takes pride in being objective in studying some aspect of behavior. Only in this way can he unearth the causes and effects of various behaviors, which he hopes to know so that he can help people who cannot function well because of deficiencies, anxieties, or loss of contact with reality. The knowledge of the psychologist is derived both from laboratory research and from clinical experience with retarded or mentally disturbed persons, as well as with healthy persons. The area of his special competence is behavior, an area which includes not only external actions but also internal behaviors, such as brain functions and hormone effects and, for humans at least, thought processes and patterns of feelings.

Although religion is manifest in many facets of life—in art, in politics, in education, in business, in the everyday dealings of persons with one another—its distinguishing characteristic is its concern with God. Hence, the study of religion is called *theology*, that is, the science of God. It proceeds in a very different way from other sciences because its subject, God, is not immediately available for observation or experimentation. Theology is a purely mental science that builds systems of thought on the basis of revelation, which is information that God has made known about himself. Christian theology also bases much on history because it believes that the ultimate revelation was made in the historical life, deeds, and sayings of Jesus of Nazareth.

The great problem in theology today is defining the revelation on which it is based. Present-day theologians recognize that such sources of revelation as the Bible do not give a direct image of God revealing himself so much as they give the thoughts of men who felt they had in one way or another experienced or understood something about God. The contemporary theologian is apt to look for revelation not only in the traditional sources like the Bible and church teachings but also in the present experience of believers who feel that they have grasped something of God as did prophets or saints of long ago. God is revealing himself, says contemporary theology, in the life experiences of people today. Finding God in one's life and believing in him gives one a theological view of things that affords deeper insight into the mystery of the universe and oneself, that gives new impetus to loving involvement with other persons, and that promises a salvation beyond death.

The initial encounter of psychology and religion was very unpleasant. In their clinical experience psychologists often found religious ideas at the center of a patient's anxieties or delusions. The average person would be stunned by the number of persons in mental hospitals whose interviews include something like this:

PSYCHOLOGIST: Do you keep track of the news while you're here?

PATIENT: No. I keep track of something else.

PSYCHOLOGIST: What do you keep track of?

PATIENT: I keep track of Jesus.

PSYCHOLOGIST: How do you keep track of him?

PATIENT: He talks to me. From the other side of the wall. I stand by the wall and listen.

PSYCHOLOGIST: What does he say?

PATIENT: He says . . .

Today a psychologist would not be surprised by such an interview because he knows that he is dealing not with a typical religious outlook but with the religious behavior of a disturbed personality. A person's religion is part of his personality, and when the personality is disturbed, religion is likely to be distorted along with everything else. It seems, though, that religion plays an unusually large role in such a vast number of cases that something about religion itself, at least the religion in our culture, seems to be especially appealing as a theatre for mental illnesses. Maybe it is because religion tolerates and has even gone so far as to canonize eccentric behaviors. At any rate, some early psychologists were very alarmed and quickly launched attacks against religion.

Religion responded with attacks on psychologists. Psychology was treated as a new form of paganism, and psychologists were regarded as the priests of the new religion. Their work, especially psychoanalysis, was considered an expensive pagan form of spiritual guidance. Some people who used to go to clergymen with their problems began going to psychologists. Many theologians considered it a mortal sin for a Catholic to go to an analyst. In addition to the anti-religious bias of the psychologists, the churches pointed to their interest in sex, which was a disreputable subject for the churches as much as for the rest of society at the time.

Barely more than ten years ago, the smoke between religion and psychology began clearing. Clergymen began recognizing the value of psychological findings and techniques for their own work. Psychology courses were rapidly introduced into seminary programs. Psychological tests became a regular part of evaluating candidates for the ministry or religious life. Moral teachings were re-examined in the light of psychological data. Clergymen were trained to use psychological techniques in counseling their parishioners. Psychologists, for their part, began recognizing that not all religion is destructive of personality and that it may even be enhancing. An intense interest in religious development and in the role of religion in personality characterizes contemporary American psychology.

It must be admitted that, despite the signs of change, in some segments of the churches and in some psychological circles large residues of mutual distrust remain. This hostility can be overcome only if psychology and religion each recognizes its limits. Psychology must acknowledge that as a science it cannot comment on the basic questions about life that religion tries to answer, and it certainly cannot promise any salvation from the limits of human existence. Religion must acknowledge that it cannot heal: The disturbed personality is disturbed in religion as in other aspects of living, and efforts to resolve a problem by intensifying one's piety are more likely to increase than to diminish the disturbance. Neither psychology nor religion can do the other's job.

Thought and Discussion: (1) Does the psychologist have the right to classify religion as a form of behavior and to study it that way? (2) How does the theologian know about God? What problems does he have in being sure of his knowledge? (3) Why is so much strange behavior linked to religion? (4) What do psychology and religion have in common?

Religion and the Individual

A simple statement that all religious people are good or that all religious people are bad would be naive. Most of us today would not think too highly of the pious men who organized inquisitions and, for the glory of God, burned non-believers at the stake, nor of the indulgence salesmen who conned the poor of Europe to pay for the art treasures of Rome. On the other hand, we must acknowledge the religious sentiment that led a Damian to devote his life to the outcast lepers of Molokai, a Martin Luther King to champion civil rights by non-violence, and so many others, some famous and many unknown, to sacrifice themselves for others.

Religion does not exist off by itself like a cloud floating in the sky. It exists only in people. In the end, then, we must ask how religion is affecting this person or that one. Is religion making this person a righteous, cold, mechanical person like the pharisees of the New Testament and the Puritans of the seventeenth century? Is he possibly using religion as an escape from responsibilities or from life's challenges? Does his religion make him think of himself as rotten and worthless? Or is his religion making him more sensitive to others, more open to life, and more sure of his own worth? These are the questions we must answer, in terms of individuals, to assess the impact of religion on personality.

The way people use religion depends to some extent on what needs they feel most keenly. People who have a strong need for security may have a religious outlook that centers around confidence in God and reliance on clergymen, who are accepted as God's representatives. A strong need for meaning may generate a religion that is very theological: religious thinking may predominate over feelings or behavior. Where there is a great need for closure one may find the religion highly moralistic, with emphasis on divine rewards and punishments at the end of history.

The theologian recognizes these different religious constellations in revelation itself where, for example, the Gospel of St. John is seen to be the work of a very speculative person, the Gospel of St. Matthew the work of a moralistic person, and the Gospel of St. Luke the work of a person most preoccupied with the promise of salvation for the poor of the earth. Similar variations in emphasis can be found in the scriptures of other religions, reflecting the individuals who contributed to the body of sacred literature. If we find these differences in the authors of revelation, it is no surprise that we find them in ordinary believers. As a matter of fact, it suggests that even within the same church we should expect to find religious differences.

Churches vary in how much religious differences they tolerate among their members. While some churches allow their members a wide range of beliefs and practices, other churches tend to set rather narrow limits. But a church cannot control what people believe; it can only control who is allowed to remain in the church. Most churches teach that the conscience of the individual is sovereign. This is an acknowledgment that a person's religion should be affected by and be consistent with his individual personality. It could not be otherwise because, whether a church recognizes it or not, a person's religious outlook is bound to be influenced by his individual upbringing, his experiences, and his need structure. As long as no two people are exactly the same, no two people will have exactly the same religion. Similarities in religious behaviors might be achieved, but on the more important levels of thought and feeling, individual differences will remain.

Religion might or might not be integrated into the rest of one's personality. A person may go to church regularly, belong to church organizations, voice total acceptance of a creed—in short, have all the credentials of a religious person—and yet not allow his religion to affect the way he thinks and feels and behaves when he is not at a church function. Moreover, his religion may have no part in his relationship to his family, his attitude toward his work and business practices, or his everyday pattern of living. In this case, the individual's religion is not integrated into the rest of his personality. Instead, his religion is sealed off in a little compartment by itself and is taken out for display only on Sundays or other religious occasions.

The trouble with a non-integrated religious sentiment is that it does not do much for the person. It may make him look good before the neighbors, or he may believe that just carrying out certain routines will get him some kind of salvation after death. But the power of religion to transform personality and to contribute toward fulfillment here and now is locked up. The person is like a miser who has something valuable but gets nothing out of it.

The theologian as much as the psychologist believes that religion should be integrated into the rest of personality. A person's religion should affect the way he habitually thinks and feels and behaves. It should be reflected in his attitude toward other people, toward his work or business, toward social issues. Religion gets beyond social decoration and useless ritualism only when it is integrated into the rest of one's personality.

Once the barrier between religion and the rest of personality is leveled, both are free to influence each other. Consequently, the person whose religion is more open to the rest of his personality will probably have a more individualistic religion. He may not believe or practice all that other church members do. He may have some personal religious views that others would consider unusual (or heretical, if they are going to be nasty about it). The price that religion must pay if it is going to influence everyday life is that it, in turn, must be ready to be influenced by the experiences of everyday life. In the integrated person, religion changes a person's living, and his living changes his religion.

Thought and Discussion: (5) How much does your church tolerate individual differences? (6) Should a church allow its members to believe and practice what they want? Should people be excluded for being heretics? (7) Do all people tend to accept some of a church's teachings and to reject others? Is it good to have an all-or-nothing attitude in belonging to a church? (8) Do we tend to think less of a person whose life experiences lead him to reject certain religious practices as useless or certain religious beliefs as untrue?

Unhealthy Religion

First we shall illustrate how the religion of some individuals can be damaging to their human development, then how religion can be enhancing. Religion is unhealthy when it is used as an escape or a cover-up for personal conflicts, when it is used to manipulate people, when it creates anxieties where there are no rational conflicts, when it undermines self-esteem, and when it inflicts unnecessary physical destruction.

Today we find the churches intensely interested in social problems such as poverty, race, and war. Perhaps some of this interest is a reaction to the charges that have been leveled against religion as having encouraged an attitude of escape from the world. The religion of just a few decades ago was rather other-worldly. It preached that the religious person is just a pilgrim on earth, an exile far from his true kingdom. It emphasized God's control, not man's control over events on the face of the earth. An attitude of "God wills it" or "God will provide" sometimes enabled the pious person to escape responsibility for injustices and disasters. For example, the Christian slave traders of the New World justified their business by referring to the biblical story of Noah cursing his sons, in which one part of mankind (one of Noah's sons) was condemned to be slaves to the rest. Since it was God's will that part of mankind be slaves, no good Christian could get upset about it. The caste system in India, which continues to prevail although it has been legally abolished, likewise is based on the belief that

God destined some people to be well-off and others to be miserably poor, and therefore no religious person need think of trying to change the lot of the poor. Not long ago, Christian marriage manuals encouraged parents to keep on having more children, even if they could not properly take care of the ones they already had, because God would provide. At one time or another, most religions, both Christian and non-Christian, have not only excused but blessed wars. In short, there is a tendency to use religion to justify policies that cannot be justified on human grounds. Any religion, however, that makes God accountable for human behavior degrades both God and man.

There are many ways religion can be used as a cover-up. The person whose daily life lacks the charity that religions preach may consider himself a good person because he prays or goes to church. In our culture there is often a suppression of affection, evident in a lack of intimacy between parents and children, which is sometimes explained by a particular brand of religion that exalts a cold, puritanical ideal of parenthood. Religious celibacy is sometimes a cover-up for an excessive attachment to a parent or for an unhealthy attitude towards sexuality.

Religion can also be used to manipulate or intimidate people. Parents or clergymen who use religion to intimidate children or parishioners into doing their will provide the most obvious examples of religious manipulation. But there are more subtle forms, like religious prejudice. A society can manipulate a whole group of people into a disadvantageous position on the basis of their religion. Although the classic example is the stereotype forced on Jews, other examples are readily available, like the role of social inferiors imposed on Catholics in Northern· Ireland or on non-Catholics in Spain.

Another way in which religion can be unhealthy is in creating anxieties that are without rational justification. Anxieties are not always avoidable, nor are they always needless. For example, people often experience the anxiety of having to make difficult moral choices; these choices, however, can be made on rational grounds without the pressure of religious *taboos*.

A taboo is a prohibition for which there is no reasoned explanation; it is simply said that such and such is against God's will, and that is supposed to end the discussion. Sexual taboos seem to have an especially large role in religion. Sexual taboos had gone so far, in medieval Christianity, for example, as to prohibit any intercourse between a man and his wife under threat of damnation. Hence, all children were born from sin. Although sexual taboos are a bit more restrained today, they are still very evident.

Anxieties induced by religion also occur in the already painful process of dying. A religion that puts most of its stress on ideas like divine judgment and retribution after death not only panics little children but greatly aggravates the emotional shock of the dying. Many teenagers, too, seem to pass through a phase when they are anxious about dying, and during this emotional crisis religion may be more threatening than relieving.

Closely related to these anxieties are concepts of guilt and self-esteem. There is a healthy guilt which leads a person to recognize that he has done some harm. There is another kind of guilt that is unhealthy: a guilt that either exaggerates the harm that has been done or imposes penances that injure the person or holds a person responsible for something he did not do. Barring special circumstances, it would be neurotic for a father to hold himself responsible for his son's death because he allowed him to use the car in which he was killed, for a woman to think she is going to be damned because she did not go to church on a stormy Sunday, or for a person to go without eating for a day because he told a lie. A guilt that imposes mental or physical punishments where none are due, or where they are excessive, reinforces unrealistic attitudes that interfere with effective living.

Sometimes a religion tends to undermine a person's self-esteem. It teaches him to think of himself as a miserable sinner who is born with a corrupted human nature and is ever unworthy in the eyes of God. This is specifically a reformation Protestant teaching, but as religious teachings are wont to do, it has filtered into other religious outlooks also. There is nothing more important than a person's feelings toward himself. The one consistent trait of persons whose inability to cope with life brings them to a psychologist is low self-esteem, and an essential part of rehabilitation is the recovery of self-esteem. A person needs to think well of himself, and religion, therefore, should not be degrading but encouraging.

Besides the psychological damage an unhealthy religion can cause, there are sometimes physical harms resulting from religious practices. Religious writers have been full of praise for the saint who slept on fragments of broken glass, for the saint who supposedly refused his mother's breast as an infant, for the saint who wore tin underwear on cold days, for the saint who beat himself until the blood ran. Such so-called penances are not often encountered these days, but the attitude behind them persists. The primitive concept of sacrifice, which very much needs to be reexamined, survives in the religious education of children, in the preaching of clergymen, and in official doctrines of churches. The notion is conveyed that when people impose suffering on themselves God is made happy. Religious people are taught that pain is good, maybe even the road to salvation. While religion might usefully engender an attitude of looking for meaning in unavoidable suffering, it is quite another thing to go looking for suffering. Self-mutilation in the name of religion points to a sick religion.

Thought and Discussion: (9) Does religion engender a leave-it-to-God attitude? (10) How and why do certain ideas eventually come to be regarded as the "will of God"? (11) Does religion tend to teach the suppression of emotions, such as affection and hostility? (12) When is "self-sacrifice" good and when is it not?

Healthy Religion

A healthy religion enhances personality. It stimulates growth and helps one toward fulfillment. A religion is healthy when it gives meaning to a person's life, reinforces values, gives a person a better understanding of himself, and stimulates ecstatic experiences.

Perhaps the greatest advantage of religion is that it helps a person discover meaning for his life. In our age of automation when we seem to be in danger of being absorbed into the mass of machines we have surrounded ourselves with, the need for meaning seems more acute than ever before. A person has to feel that he is more than a complicated computer or a disposable container.

An empirical science, however, can offer no other view of human nature because science begins with the premise that everything is accessible to investigation and subject to laws. Research and experimentation lose their validity if science abandons its view of man as anything more than a bio-chemical system capable of learning. For example, medical research which allows for something mysterious in human nature, let us call it "X", will never discover if a disease is cured by a new medicine or by "X", unless it is agreed that "X" does nothing, in which case it is a meaningless concept anyway. It is self-defeating, then, for science to admit that there is "something mysterious" in human nature. It would not be able to predict how the organism would respond to chemicals (such as medicines) or to various situations (such as love). Everyday life depends on being able to predict how humans are likely to react.

Still the scientist, like others, does not usually think of himself as a mere bio-chemical system. He believes his life is not entirely measurable. Every man seeks another dimension not only to his own life but to the entire world. Moreover, he finds it difficult to imagine that even death could annihilate his living, his loving, or himself. The feeling that there is a meaning to the universe and to one's individual life seems to be an essential characteristic of the self-fulfilling person. These meanings science cannot give to man. Religion, however, is not bound by the observable. It can look and hope beyond appearances.

Religion also teaches and reinforces values by which persons relate to one another and fulfill themselves. There may not be any values that exist solely because of religion; the same values seem to exist outside of religion. Yet religion gives an added weight to values. It would be a painful process both for the individual and for society if everyone had to learn values through his own experiences. As it is, religious teachings on values incorporate the experiences of countless generations and facilitate the individual's striving for fulfillment.

Another way religion enhances a person is by encouraging him to form a realistic image of himself. The ability to see oneself is called *self-objectification.* A person should be able to sort of detach himself from himself and look at himself from the outside, not with the unconscious detachment of a split personality but with the conscious detachment of a person who is concerned about what he is becoming. To some extent each person is his own creator. We have choices to make most of the time, and these choices leave their effects on us. Our choices help to make us what we are. It is good for a person to look into the mirror of his mind to see what he is making of himself. It is characteristic of immature and disturbed persons that they have little skill in self-objectification; they hold distorted views of themselves. The mature and self-fulfilling person, on the other hand, has become so because he is able to be self-objective. He is conscious of what he is becoming by his choices.

Religion prompts a person to see himself from God's viewpoint. If God is conceived of as a loving father, or at least as a benevolent creator, the individual may grow in self-esteem as well as self-objectification. A person learns to see himself as something very special and precious, unique and good because of the love that God has invested in making him. The Christian doctrines of the incarnation, of God becoming man, and of the redemption of each person by the death of the God-man, add an infinite sum to the value of each person. The religious person who meditates on these beliefs is bound to grow in self-esteem and in his relationships with other persons.

An aspect of religion that tends to be overlooked is its orientation toward ecstatic experience. Mysticism of one kind or another is held in honor by all religions. The mystic who seems to have some kind of experience that lifts him out of himself and puts him in touch with the universe excites the admiration of his fellow believers. Of the Western

religions Catholicism especially has created a special place
for the mystic by founding monasteries for contemplatives.
The worship rituals of religions, moreover, have mystical
experience for all believers as one of their goals.

It seems strange that mysticism should attract so little
attention, apart from an interest in Eastern religions on
the part of some youths, in an age when the quest for experiences takes many forms, ranging from drug usage to stereo-
phonic self-bombardment. What people are searching for
so desperately is an essential part of being human—it is the
experience of oneself. Such experiences which seem at once
to lift a person out of himself and to make him fully in touch
with himself, which seem to lift him above the universe and
at the same time immerse him in it, have been found to be a
distinguishing trait of people who are unusually happy and
fulfilled.

One psychologist who made a special study of excep-
tionally happy and self-fulfilling people has pointed out
that these peak experiences can result from ordinary circumstances. They can be experienced by a housewife who
delights in cooking a special meal or by a man who enjoys
having a little garden in his backyard. The important thing
is that a person have some experience of himself either
through being creative or experiencing someone else's
creativity or somehow becoming totally aware of himself.
The exhilaration and freedom that a person feels in floating off a ski run or standing at the top of a skyscraper seem
to carry over and lend a greater exhilaration and freedom to
the more ordinary moments of daily living. Worship, too,
should offer such moments of ecstasy when a person is lifted
beyond himself into union with God. Prayer and worship
fall short if they fail to give this liberating, God-touching
sensation.

Thought and Discussion: (13) Should we have a purge of the saints? (14) Can a person fulfill his need for meaning in life without religion? (15) What picture of yourself do you get from your religion? (16) Why do the upper-class churches downplay religious experience while lower-class churches, like storefront churches, emphasize it? Is there more freedom, spontaneity, and individuality in lower-class churches?

Images of God

The human personality is always a great mystery; it is very complex, immersed in the history of the individual, open to new possibilities. The personality of God is, of course, an even greater mystery. We have only fragmentary, indirect knowledge of God. Hence it would be impossible to "analyze" the personality of God. But the images people have of God are something else. They are human concepts, and they can be analyzed. It is these human images of God which will be discussed here.

The Book of Genesis says that God made man in his own image and likeness. The reverse is also true. Man makes God in his own image and likeness. If God has revealed anything definite about himself, he has revealed so little that man cannot resist the temptation to fill in the image with features of his own design. For example, we are constantly referring to God as if God were sexual. The usual pronoun for God is "he" rather than "it." The attribution of masculinity to God is, of course, a human preference. We could just as readily find reasons to make God female and refer to God as "she." Many religions have preferred to think of God as a female. In the Bible, Isaiah pictures God as the mother of Israel. However, where women were regarded as inferior to men, the masculine image of God was bound to prevail. This is but a glimpse of how the culture influences our concepts of the personality of God.

The images of God that are commonly entertained are not all very flattering to God. They mean to be, yet they fail by their extravagance and inconsistency. We are much too quick in saying this or that of God, so that we say too much and end up with an image rather like the ancient Mesopotamian statues with the body of a lion, the head of a man, the wings of an eagle, and various other parts. Furthermore, the images tend to outlast the particular cultures which generate them and to be carried over into an age where they no longer make sense. A good illustration of this is the concept of God based on medieval culture which still hangs on today in a culture where it is no longer flattering but obnoxious.

In a typical medieval society, the lord lived in a castle up on a mountainside overlooking his villages. He controlled the lives of all his subjects—granting each villager a bit of land to farm, taking from each a part of his produce, providing a church for the people, regulating whatever trade there was between the village and the outside, declaring holidays, drafting youths into his service, and so on. The lord was born noble, all others being inferior to him by birth. If a peasant offended the lord, perhaps by poaching from his garden, it was a far greater crime than if it had been committed against another peasant. Another peasant might be reimbursed, but nothing a peasant could do would be sufficient to make up for a crime against the lord.

It was natural for the people of this culture to imagine God as the super-lord. St. Anselm could think of no better way to explain the incarnation and redemption than to make God the lord who was offended by his subjects, to say that the subjects could not make up for a crime against the lord, and then to have Christ come as the savior lord to make reparation to the offended lord. Maybe it just would not have made sense in the culture of those times for the offended lord to be big about it and forgive his subjects; the crime had to be punished. Our culture still features a penal system rather than a corrective system. The Middle Ages, however, had a legal concept we no longer consider just: an innocent man could suffer in place of the guilty. It made no difference as long as someone suffered. So the medieval God accepted the death of Jesus as payment for the crimes of his subjects.

It is true that some aspects of these ideas go back to the Bible, for the Bible also is the product of cultures whose ideas we can challenge. For instance, we no longer accept the biblical ideal of the holy war in which the enemy, including women and children, are totally exterminated for the glory of God. Nor do we accept slavery any longer, although the New Testament teaches that slaves are supposed to be obedient to their masters.

In our contemporary culture where we believe in the equality of all men, have a little more belief in forgiveness, and would not tolerate the punishment of the innocent in place of the guilty, the medieval baron-God comes out a barbarian.

Another old but unflattering image of God which seems to hold on over the centuries is the image of God as the avenger. The notion of God as an avenger may be one of the most primitive notions of God. Vengeance was firmly established in primitive society, and the avenger of a murder or other crime was considered a hero.

It was natural, then, for God to be depicted as someone who would bring vengeance on evildoers. But even in ancient times it was recognized that this image of God is somehow inconsistent with other images of God as father, life-giver, and protector. In the biblical story of the exodus from Egypt, vengeance is taken against the Egyptian slavemasters by slaying the firstborn of all their families. Although the biblical writer attributed this act to God, he could not bring himself to make God directly the killer, and so he provided God with an agent called "the angel of death" to do the deed. But this ploy cleared his image of God no more than a modern mob leader is cleared by using a henchman to do his dirty work.

The essential difficulty with the image of God as avenger is that vengeance itself is a primitive moral act which offers no creative solution to a moral situation but only adds evil to evil. Although vengeance was regarded as highly moral throughout most of the history of mankind, it is no longer regarded as moral in our culture. Our society forbids vengeance and calls instead for the rehabilitation of the wrongdoer. The God who avenges is not only out-of-date but immoral by modern standards.

Besides the medieval baron-God and the primitive avenger God, there are at least a half-dozen other divine comic-book monsters on parade in the popular imagination. It is the task of the theologian to expose these frauds. They are too many to unmask here, but the worst one should be mentioned—the sadistic one, that is, the one that enjoys watching people suffer. This one generally turns up at disaster scenes and in hospital wards as the God who willed the suffering; he also turns up in theology as the God who designed life as a trial, with lots of little trials within it, like the psychopathic maniac who starts chopping bits off his dog to see how much he has to cut off before his dog stops loving him. If he chops off so much that the dog dies before biting him, then it was a good dog. And if a man can accept the trials presumably designed by God and go all the way to death without rebelling, then he is a good man. This psychotic image of God is offered as merely one example of how the greatest sicknesses and perversions of human beings can be attributed to God. Such false notions of God need to be recognized and replaced.

Many a Christian tries to draw his picture of God from Jesus. Unfortunately, as our knowledge of Jesus is also rather incomplete, we tend to fill in details by our own imagining. The portraits of Jesus that are given to us in the Gospels are more like abstract art than photographs. Each evangelist has given us a different picture of Jesus. The mystifying, melodramatic, God-conscious Jesus of St. John's Gospel looks very different from the tired, dusty roadside preacher and miracle-worker of St. Mark's Gospel, from the eloquent orator of St. Matthew's Gospel, and from the gentle, compassionate healer of St. Luke's Gospel. From these impressions of Jesus, which so much bespeak the personal characteristics of the evangelists themselves, we remain free to form any number of different images of Jesus, ranging from the sugar-coated Jesus of the calendars to the severe Jesus of oriental mosaics.

Maybe the message that God wants to convey about himself he has conveyed by saying so little. It is not very likely that God's silence has been due to an oversight on his part. The problem of finding adequate images for God is the most difficult problem for the theologian.

Thought and Discussion: (17) How would you describe God? (18) What images of God were you taught? What images show up most commonly in preaching? (19) Would you call God a person? (There is a theological-philosophical sense

in which God is a "person," as three, but this has little to
do with the usual meaning of the word.) (20) What do the
images of Jesus in your home and in your church suggest?
What does the crucifix suggest?

Summary

Psychology is the study of behavior. Its overriding
purpose is to help persons toward fulfillment. Religion is
concerned with the impact of God on man and on man's life.
The initial encounter of psychology with religion was charac-
terized by some hostility on both sides. Each seemed to be
intruding on the other's domain. But religion cannot heal,
and psychology cannot save. Religion affects each individual
personality in a different way. No two persons are the same,
with the consequence that no two persons have exactly the
same religious feelings, attitudes, or outlooks. An unhealthy
religious outlook is one that keeps a person from facing himself and from accepting responsibility, one that creates ir-
rational anxieties, undermines self-esteem, or engenders
harm to oneself. A healthy religious outlook is one that
gives meaning to a person's life, inculcates values that help
a person toward fulfillment, helps a person see what he is
becoming, and provides moments of ecstasy. Central to a
religion is its concept of God. Our various concepts of God
need to be carefully examined both for what they imply
about God himself and for what they imply about God's
relationship to man.

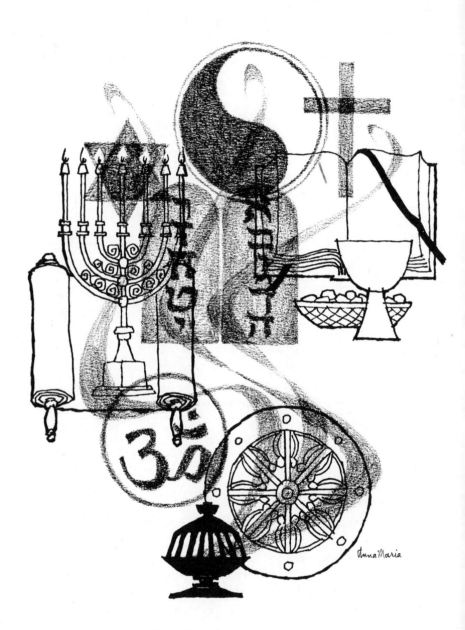

Chapter 4

Mature Religion

We are still exploring religion insofar as it is a personal trait. Religion in the sense of organized churches will be examined in the next chapter. As a personal trait religion is very difficult to define. It ranges over a wide array of thought, feeling, and behavior patterns. For simplicity's sake we can divide religion into four components: religious beliefs, religious rituals, religious experiences, and religious morality. This will give us an outline for describing religion in its mature form.

A person should be willing to examine the maturity of his religion. Being an adult does not guarantee religious maturity. One can fail to grow in religion as in other aspects of personality by not allowing it to be changed as he grows in knowledge, in experiences of life, and in self-understanding. The temptation is strong for an adult who is busy with many things to regress to the religion of a child. Religious maturing requires moments of serious, honest thinking which may frighten the person who has never really thought through his religion before. The prospect of discovering that one's religion may be in some ways immature and in need of change understandably exasperates the person who thought he had settled his religious convictions once and for all. Indeed many Catholics have been upset in recent years because their church has forced some changes upon them. But openness to change is necessary for any kind of maturity, religious or otherwise.

Religious Beliefs

To some people beliefs are the crux of religion. What separates the religious person from the non-religious in this view is not so much pious practices or morals as beliefs. The hero is the martyr who chooses to die rather than deny his faith.

The Jews from the time of the Machabeean War (second century B.C.) and the Christians until the end of the Middle Ages put much stock in the expression of true beliefs. The primary goal of the great ecumenical councils was to produce creeds which stated beliefs in exact language. In times of persecution the believer was expected to state his faith publicly and bravely unto death. Those who did were honored as martyrs, and their graves became places of worship. The attraction of becoming a martyr became so great that the Christian bishops of northern Africa had to decree it a grave sin for a person to purposely expose himself to the persecuting authorities.

What of the person who really believed his religion but lied to the persecutors to save his life? He was considered a fallen man and expelled from the church. To avoid this calamity many men fled into the wilderness during the irregular flare-ups of persecution, and some stayed on to form the beginnings of the religious life as we know it today. After the period of persecutions was over, the Christian churches spent many years debating what should be done with their fallen members, for they seem to have been very numerous. Finally it was decided to readmit them to the churches after they had done suitable penances—frequently lasting for many years—and then as second-class members who might have to stay segregated in the back of the church during services for the rest of their lives.

With so much emphasis on true beliefs, it was a logical turn of events for the persecuted to become the persecutors in subsequent centuries. The racks and iron virgins of the Inquisition maintained the tradition of true beliefs. Although the Protestant churches which emerged from the Reformation had different beliefs from the church of Rome, they put the same emphasis on true beliefs and soon established their own systems of beliefs.

Another historical effect of the early Christian emphasis on true beliefs was the *rigor mortis* of beliefs. The threat was too great for anyone to seriously challenge beliefs. To merely memorize the creeds and to downplay any intellectual analysis was the safest course. We are inclined to think of the Christian faith of the Middle Ages as very intellectual, represented by St. Thomas Aquinas; as a matter of fact, he met with condemnations in his own times, and his writings did little other than gather dust until he was "discovered" at the dawn of the modern period.

The *rigor mortis* of beliefs resulted in their remaining the same while the culture on which they were based decayed and was replaced by another culture, so that some of the beliefs no longer had much meaning. The great masses of the faithful abandoned their beliefs to the clergy, who alone were considered competent to understand them. The ordinary believer was supposed to be an empty vase into which the clergy could pour true beliefs—the believer himself was not expected to do any thinking. As for the clergy, neither did they do much theologizing; seminaries were sometimes notorious for their poor education. Clergy were trained to know the content of a few safe old theology manuals. Toward the end of the nineteenth century and the beginning of the twentieth century, for example, when some of the intellectuals began a scholarly study of the Bible, the best Catholic Scripture scholars were forbidden to teach or publish anything, and some were forced out of the church. Liberal interpreters of the Bible did not fare much better in the Protestant churches. Bans and censorship on Scripture scholars and other theologians are still being maintained in some churches to protect the faithful.

It would seem, though, that the mature believer is one who understands his faith, not one who delegates it to somebody else to understand. The idea that the faith might be too difficult for the ordinary believer and should therefore be delegated to clergy or theologians would come as a shock to Moses, Jesus, Buddha, Mohammed, and other religious founders who seem to have felt that their message was for the ordinary man. If their teachings are now too difficult for ordinary people, something unfortunate must have happened to their teachings over the centuries.

It falls upon the believer, if he is going to be a mature believer, to examine first of all the truth of his beliefs. When the Vatican dropped certain saints from the liturgical calendar, one of the priest-scholars on the official commission responsible for the changes explained: "Certain saints came to be popular because of very beautiful legends which have been created around their names without any guarantee that they existed, such as Saints Dorothy, Christopher, Barbara, and Catherine of Alexandria. They have been dropped from the official calendar. The Christian people cannot be officially asked to pray except in truth."

Praying to saints who never existed may hardly seem

reasonable, but many Christians still would not abandon their St. Christopher medals and statues. Neither will many believers allow their reason to upset cherished beliefs about God, about the world, about churches, or about life after death. It is amazing, for instance, how long religious people kept on referring to evolution as only a scientific theory that we might intelligently reject.

Besides examining beliefs for their truth, the mature believer should examine beliefs for the effects they have upon him. A good illustration is religious beliefs about chosen people. Reading ancient Near Eastern literature and stone inscriptions, one gets the idea that every little kingdom thought of itself as God's chosen people. Since the Israelites were most careful about preserving their beliefs in writing, and since the Christians took over many Jewish ideas for themselves, we commonly think of Israel as God's chosen people. Christians, then, think of themselves as the new chosen people. This belief in being a chosen people has spawned an unending stream of prejudices for at least the past 3,000 years. It has set Jews against gentiles, and Christians against Jews and so-called pagans. Despite the efforts of Jews and Christians who were convinced of the brotherhood of all men, the ranks of Jews and Christians have been infected with an attitude of religious superiority that paved the way for such atrocities as the Nazi concentration camps.

It made headlines the world over when Pope John XXIII, celebrating the midnight vigil for Easter, cut out the words in the service that slandered the Jews. His plain humanity enabled him to recognize an odious religious sentiment even when it occurred in the official worship of his church. Likewise, every mature believer must examine his own beliefs for the attitudes they encourage, to see whether his beliefs are making him a better person or a worse person.

Besides the contents of a person's beliefs, the style of a person's believing tends to have marked effects on his personality. Whether a person believes one thing or another, he can believe it in a flexible open-minded way or in a rigid closed-minded way. The open-minded person is receptive to the impact of his experiences of life and the experiences of others. He modifies his beliefs as he learns more from living. The closed-minded person insulates himself against his own experiences of life and against the impact of others who interact with him. He is an unchanging person. One psychological study of a large group of clergymen looked into the relationships between their theological beliefs and their scores on a self-actualization inventory. As might be expected, the conservative believers were more sure of their roles as clergymen and had higher self-regard, but they were also less self-actualizing, more dependent people, more rigid, more insensitive, more negative in their views of human nature, and poorer in interpersonal relationships. However, it should be remembered that the dogmatic style of thinking is not limited to those who think conservatively. It is also possible for a person with liberal views to be very dogmatic in the style of his believing.

Religious doubt may be the sign of a strong believer more often than of a weak believer. The person who never examines his beliefs is not likely to have religious doubts. It is the person whose religious beliefs are open to reflection who encounters difficulties, but it is only by working them out that he refines his beliefs. The religious upset often experienced in adolescence is due in part to the final maturation of intelligence, for the ability to do abstract thinking develops at about age sixteen. When the mind is fully alive and one is sensitive to how beliefs are affecting his life, religious search may be more common than religious certainty.

Thought and Discussion: (1) Does a person become less open to change as he grows older? If so, why? (2) Should religious beliefs be determined by the clergy? (3) Are most believers simply passive receptacles who accept without question whatever their churches preach? (4) Besides the chosen people concept, what are some other religious beliefs that have given rise to harmful attitudes?

Religious Rituals

Here we are using the phrase religious rituals to include any devotions or pious practices that a person performs as part of his religion, whether these religious acts are done in private or in public with other worshipers. The variety of behaviors that may be rituals in one religion or another is practically unlimited. The seven prayers a day of the Moslem, the unclipped beard of a Hasidic Jew, the self-torture of a Hindu *fakir*, the yoga of a Zen Buddhist, the animal sacrifice of an East African, the cross worn by a Christian—all these are ritual behaviors. Most religious people perform some rituals, which may both express and further strengthen their beliefs.

The mature worshiper is one who gets something worthwhile out of his rituals. His opposite is the person who goes through rituals without getting anything out of them; maybe he is just responding to the conditioning of childhood training or to social pressures. Or maybe he carries out the ritual because his religion makes it a sin not to do so. It would seem, though, that a religious ritual has a value for a person only if he gets from it some insights or feelings that enhance his attitudes toward himself or other people. In other words, they make him a better person.

Sometimes one hears a religious person say that rituals are valid even if he gets nothing out of them because worship is supposed to be for God, not for man. Such a viewpoint presents a grave problem for the theologian. The concept of God is so constructed that in most religions it is impossible for God to get anything out of whatever humans may do. God can neither benefit nor suffer from human behavior because God is infinitely self-sufficient and unchangingly perfect and fulfilled in every way. It is because God cannot be affected in any way by man that theologians refer to God's relationship to man as a relationship of *grace*, that is, a relationship of loving that man is not able to merit or earn.

As long as this concept of God and this concept of grace prevail, to be consistent with himself the religious person will have to acknowledge that religious rituals are for man's benefit at the same time as they are for the worship of God. Their value for the worshiper, moreover, depends on what attitudes he has towards them and on how they affect him. Rituals which do not make a person better are useless. Christianity goes further than other religions in teaching that worship is for man's benefit. Christianity teaches that its highest forms of worship, the Sacraments, will cease to exist when man no longer needs them in the kingdom of God.

Immature worship—what the theologian calls superstitious worship—is not hard to document. The Old Testament prophets breathed thunder and lightning against worshipers who sacrificed animals or burned grain offerings without becoming any better themselves. In the Mass, bells are still rung for the lifting up of the consecrated bread and wine. The bells were originally rung to summon the chatting noblemen from the church steps to come in to view the elevations. Then they would leave to go off in their carriages to some other church for the same performance because they believed that just looking at the consecrated bread and wine removed all their sins. Their rituals were a substitute for self-change rather than a stimulus. Little need be said about the similar extraordinary promises associated with certain medals, scapulars, and devotions to which miraculous powers are attributed or which are supposed to guarantee salvation.

Historically, misguided parish clergy and religious groups have gone to extremes in promoting religious goods and devotions, sometimes for financial reasons. In medieval times, for example, monasteries trained Mass-saying priests whose sole function was to say repeated Masses for the dead in return for stipends to support the monasteries. This was done despite the fact that official Catholic teaching holds each Mass has infinite value. Church law put a small brake on such practices by limiting the number of Masses a priest could say on one day. But some Catholics still allocate large sums of money for Masses for the dead in the belief that the more Masses said for them the better off they will be in the world beyond.

Rituals help a person grow when they strengthen worthwhile values or beliefs, or offer opportunities for religious experiences that increase his self-awareness. Having a beard, wearing a medal, or dressing a certain way may remind a person of values to which he has dedicated himself or of religious beliefs which help him find fulfillment. Church services usually underline these beliefs and values and relate them to contemporary situations. By bringing worshipers together in the same place they also provide for a mutual sharing and reinforcement of religious outlooks. Prayer especially leads a person to get a better view of himself, his situation in the world, and his relations to others, and thus helps him to become a more fulfilled person.

The value of a ritual, then, lies not in the ritual itself but in its effect on a person. The ritual itself may be like a Quaker prayer meeting at which the worshipers all pray silently with hardly a word ever spoken, or like an Orthodox Jewish service conducted in a language which many of the worshipers do not understand, or an elaborate ceremony like a papal Mass. The ritual may take the form of a spectacle which the worshipers behold or a series of activities which they perform. What is better depends on the individual personality of the worshiper, for some get more out of attending while others get more out of participating. In turn, the individual's preference and the kind of ritual that means most to him are usually a reflection of the religious tradition in which he was raised. A church becomes part of a person, and he becomes part of it.

Thought and Discussion: (5) Can a person be religious without having any religious rituals? Are there such people? (6) Do your rituals make you a better person? How? (7) What would you respond to a person who says, "I don't go to church because I don't get anything out of it"? (8) What difficulties do individuals have when a church changes its rituals? What should individuals do if they get less out of new rituals?

Religious Experiences

To speak of religious experiences is to go into the area of feelings. A modern Anglo-Saxon culture like that of the United States is an anti-feeling culture. We are taught to respect cool reason and to frown on passion. Strong feelings are taboo. Even between many parents and their children strong feelings tend not to be expressed—except for occasional anger. The cultural bias quite naturally shows up in religion, which is expected to be highly rational and practical, devoted to such enterprises as education, hospitals, and social work. Only churches of groups who have never been integrated into the mainstream of American culture, such as the storefront churches of ghetto groups and the hillside churches of the poor in destitute rural areas, allow much feeling in their services. The big churches of the successful Americans prefer orderliness and restraint in both the clergy and the congregation. The preaching is subdued, and the services do not deviate from the fairly detailed pattern worked out beforehand. Only minimal movement is allowed. A very restricted range of musical styles and instruments is accepted. The character of the major churches' services is well expressed in the rigid alignments of their narrow pews.

The tourist is sometimes surprised to find that in European cathedrals dating from the Middle Ages there are no pews or that a hundred-piece orchestra will be giving a concert in the cathedral. But the music lover knows that the great classical composers like Bach wrote much of their music for church services, and historians of the theatre tell us that modern drama originated in the churches of the Middle Ages. The church sanctuary would be duly outfitted with props, and costumed performers would enact the biblical stories. At St. Paul's in London the embellishments on Pentecost included swinging great pots of smoking incense across the inside of the dome and sending down a flock of white doves. Such drama and pomp seem to have survived only in papal services. If a clergyman today tries to use a film in a church service or if Duke Ellington's jazz

Mass is actually played in church, the congregation is shocked. And except for a very few way-out churches, ballet or any kind of dancing is out of the question.

Yet faded mementos of what were once spirit-filled services are embedded in our rituals. Especially in Judaism and Catholicism the trappings of yesteryear's pomp remain in the processions that are the last vestige of the sacred dances of ancient times. In most Christian services the wine remains, although so carefully minimized that it can no longer have the uplifting effect it did at such brotherhood meals as the Last Supper and at the Eucharists of the first Christians. Perhaps the element of celebration has remained most intact in the Jewish Passover meal. Whereas St. Ambrose in the fourth century wrote a song for his people to sing in church about being drunk with the Spirit, we no longer like to associate religion with being emotionally high.

Church art shares the general inhibition. The churches of ancient times and of the Middle Ages were the art galleries of the age. Most churches today are drab. Technical architectural limitations restricted the size of windows in medieval churches, but most of today's parish churches were purposely made to be dark. The newer churches that let in more light still cling to subdued colors and outmoded art styles. They have all the restraint of a bank president's office. They express not joy but anxiety, or sometimes nothing at all.

Perhaps we have been too much bound to our culture in pruning emotion from religion. The only emotion that seems to be encouraged is guilt, and it is frequently the neurotic kind of guilt that corrodes rather than enhances personality. Joy and ecstasy should be part of religion too. The word gospel means "good news," yet one hardly gets that impression in church services on Sunday.

Since the joyful forms of music, art, dance, and drama have been put out of religion, they have taken up residence in concert halls, museums, and theaters. As a result, people have learned to go out of churches for joy, beauty, and ecstasy. In these other places they may have experiences that bring them closer to God. Thus the teenager may find more religion, as he understands it, listening to his record collection than in church.

Religion is intimately associated with being alive, with birth, and with revival. In the Psalms the singer asks God to "revive my drooping spirits." In Christian baptism one is said to be "born again." The experience of revival in religion reached its peak in American culture during the nineteenth century and has declined to a practically nonexistent level since. When the famous American psychologist William James wrote his book, *The Varieties of Religious Experience*, he traced revival experiences across the religions of the East and the West, through the ancient hermits of the desert, the mystics of the Middle Ages, and the great Protestant reformers down to the revival meetings of his own day. He concluded that the sensation of becoming a new person, which religion provided for so long, seemed to bring out the best in people. It gave them a feeling of freedom and newness that freed the creative power in them.

Religion without ecstasy seems hardly a religion at all. Religion ought to renew a person and set him free. "Ecstasy" comes from the Greek words meaning "standing outside of oneself." Without the sensation of ecstasy the person drowns in the humdrum of everyday living. The fact that so many people must turn from churches to the arts for these experiences bears witness to the religious and sacred character of the arts themselves. If we could go around and monitor the experiences of people, let us say in New York City, we might find that some people have found God living a few blocks away from St. Patrick's Cathedral at the Museum of Modern Art.

Thought and Discussion: (9) The anti-feeling bias which came into American culture with the Puritans was based on the religious belief that the body and feelings are the source of sin. Do religious people still believe this? Why are feelings still downgraded by religions? (10) Are there groups in your church, for example, teenagers, who want to enliven the ritual? What reactions do they encounter? (11) Is it possible for a person to find his religious experiences entirely in the arts rather than in church? Would there be any reasonable objection to this? (12) How many of the people you know ever have any feeling of ecstasy? What do they get it from?

Religious Morality

It was once common for theologians to speak of a revealed morality. By this they meant that God made known to man through some direct communication certain moral laws. The prime example was the Ten Commandments. It was acknowledged that men could have deduced some of these laws with their own reason, but the biblical story seemed to say that God printed them on two stones and gave the stones to Moses.

Biblical scholars have long since reinterpreted the Ten Commandment story in the light of archaeological discoveries that revealed much of ancient Near Eastern culture. These commandments do not seem to have been very unique. They were the stock basics of all the Near Eastern cultures, right down to the Sabbath laws which can be traced back to Babylonian superstitions about the seventh day being unlucky and therefore no day to set about doing any work. Likewise, it was commonplace for Near Eastern peoples to make up myths about God personally writing down the laws and giving them to the ruler. This gave more weight to the laws and was an easily accepted belief since the ruler was generally regarded as God's representative anyway.

Thus, the Ten Commandments are the products of a particular culture of the second millennium B.C. It is no surprise to find Jesus in his Sermon on the Mount evaluating the Commandments as an inadequate moral code. Yet probably because the first Christians were Jews who never really gave up their Jewish ways, the Ten Commandments were carried over into Christianity and remained the basis of Christian moral instruction until just a few years ago. Of course, it was necessary to overcome the cultural limitations of the Commandments by stretching them far beyond their original meaning. Originally, the "neighbor" in these commandments meant only fellow Jews, but it was later extended to mean people of all nations. The law against adultery also was stretched to include more sexual behaviors than it behooves a pious person to know about.

With all this repair work and additions, the Ten Commandments have been kept serviceable for more than three thousand years, and even if they fade out of Christianity to be replaced by something like the Sermon on the Mount, they will continue as the moral foundation of Judaism.

The concept of a revealed morality seems to have died out. Theologians no longer point to this or that and say it is a sin because God told someone so. It is difficult to think of a single moral law which is based on a direct revelation by God. For many years religious authorities could command or condemn something by saying it was "the will of God," and this excused them from having to defend their moral codes. But with the decline of belief in a revealed morality, one must now give reasons for a moral law or prohibition, and the strength of the law is only as good as the reasons given for it. Even God is presumed to be reasonable about morality; he is not an arbitrary moral dictator.

Theologians for centuries have spoken of a natural law based on reason and knowledge of human nature. The so-called "natural law," or the law of human nature, is still the foundation of all morality. What the theologians must study to determine morality is man. The question is: What behavior patterns are fulfilling, or in accord with human nature? And, on the contrary, what behavior patterns are frustrating, or opposed to human nature? As St. Thomas Aquinas said in the thirteenth century, all morality is rooted in man's spontaneous movement toward his own happiness and fulfillment.

With human nature as the standard of morality, the theologian finds an ally in the psychologist, whose express concern is knowledge of human nature. Together they can construct principles of self-fulfillment. Only if the theologian respects the knowledge of human nature offered by the psychologist can he create a morality based on man's needs rather than on arbitrary principles. Yet religion has more to offer morality than the psychologist could give. In its beliefs religion furnishes additional motives for morality, such as belief in the brotherhood of all men and belief in the infinite value of every individual before God. It is not a matter of a new or different set of moral principles generated by religion, but of new motivation.

What has research shown about the morality of religious people? For the most part, the research data is not encouraging, but neither is it extensive so far. People who express strong religious beliefs and who belong to organized churches have not been shown to be more virtuous than other people, except in the teenage years. Religious teenagers tend to be more involved in charitable work than non-religious teenagers. Religious people have been shown to be more concerned than other people about presenting a good image of themselves. They score higher than others on psychological tests designed to measure a person's tendency to make himself appear good before other people. Religious people have more stringent and exacting moral attitudes than others; they judge more actions wrong, judge them more wrong, and are less ready to recognize extenuating circumstances. They are particularly harsh in judging acts of self-indulgence, most especially sexual behavior. Nonetheless, recent research indicates that religious people are now changing their moral attitudes as fast as others and often faster than others.

The power of religious morality does not seem to be highly visible in most ordinary believers. Yet it can be seen in extraordinary believers. It comes to the surface in the process of moral revolutions, such as that by which slavery was abolished in the Western world, and that by which capital punishment is now being challenged.

The death penalty has been accepted by society for as far back as history records. In recent years, however, it has been questioned on moral grounds as well as legal grounds. More than half of the states in the United States had already abolished the death penalty when the Supreme Court in 1972 ruled that the death penalty laws in force in the United States were illegal. So much disagreement existed among the Justices themselves that each of the nine Justices issued a separate statement about the decision. Within two years after the decision, twenty-one states had enacted new death penalty laws designed to get around the Supreme Court ruling. But even states which wanted to maintain the death penalty laws were hesitant to use them. For instance, although nearly 700 persons were on "death row" in 1974, no one had been executed in the United States since 1967. New legislation and new court cases both for and against the death penalty indicate that the debate is going to continue for some time. Yet it is clear that what nearly everybody accepted as moral for centuries is now regarded as suspect by a large part of American society.

Although members of organized religions tend to be more conforming than non-religious people, by a paradox the very strength of religion is that it liberates a person to be non-conforming. Religion liberates a person by making his primary obligation to God and not to any man. Such liberation from human authority was so evident in Jesus of Nazareth that the secular and religious leaders of Israel felt it necessary to destroy him. Jesus was an extremely independent person who refused to subordinate his convictions to the demands of the authorities. Likewise the early Christians refused to keep civil laws which they believed contradicted the law of God. For example, the early Christians all refused to serve in the military because they believed that no war could be reconciled with Christianity. Even today military service laws are testing the moral convictions of many Christians whose religious beliefs do not allow them simply to conform but require them to judge a law.

The dangers in religious morality are the same as the dangers in religious beliefs. First, there is the danger that when a moral conviction becomes part of a religion, its cultural limitations may be forgotten. Religion tends to absolutize. It also tends to hold onto cultural patterns after the culture itself has changed. In regard to the morality of war, for example, the religious moral principles of "the just war" were worked out in the Middle Ages but continue to be used today in spite of the fact that the nature of warfare has changed drastically.

Forty years ago population control was generally considered unnatural in Western culture, and all the churches went along with the culture in condemning it; when the cultural attitude toward population control changed, the churches were the slowest to recognize the change and held on longest to the old cultural attitude. In a single year, 1968, legislation was introduced in more than half the states in the U.S. to abolish the death penalty, and this certainly bears witness to a changing cultural attitude toward punishment by death. Yet religious morality continues to defend the death penalty. Many more examples could be given of the tendency of a religious sanction to embalm moral principles. The religious person must be especially aware of this moral absolutism if he is going to remain a changing, rational person.

The second danger in a religious morality is that it may become so complex, largely as a result of holding onto outmoded cultural notions, that only an elite group of experts can understand it. Consequently, the average person abandons to this elite group the responsibility for determining moral principles. This tendency is evident in the history of all the major world religions. Moslems have their moral authorities to interpret the Koran. The scribes and Pharisees were the moral experts of ancient Judaism, and Jesus' major objection to them was that they made the law too complex for the ordinary Jew to master. In Catholicism, particularly after the Protestant Reformation, a whole moral system of authorities was constructed so that a Catholic would not have to make any moral decisions for himself; all he was expected to do was to follow the opinion of a moral theologian. Even priests were trained just to know the opinions of various moral theologians. However, this tendency to abdicate personal responsibility to a group of experts is rapidly vanishing from religion, partly as a result of the greater knowledge given to the public by the mass media and partly as a result of contemporary religion's own insistence on personal freedom.

In short, mature morality has three characteristics: First, it recognizes cultural limitations and, therefore, is a changing morality; second, it is based on man's needs and is orientated toward his fulfillment; and third, it insists on personal responsibility for moral decisions. To this morality religion adds the wealth of motivations that spring from religious beliefs.

Thought and Discussion: (13) What could a religion mean by "the law of God"? How would something become "the law of God"? Is it a good idea to say that this or that moral principle comes from God? (14) Do religions generally hold onto an outmoded sexual morality? Who should determine principles of sexual morality? How should they be determined? (15) What does your religion teach about "personal conscience"? (16) Would you expect parents and teenagers to disagree on some moral principles? Is such disagreement healthy or not?

Summary

In times of persecution great emphasis was placed on stating one's faith in fixed formulas. For the past several centuries intellectual examination of Christian faith has been largely the monopoly of theologians, but in recent years the laity has become more aware of its need to understand Christianity. The mature believer is one who grapples with his faith and seeks some personal understanding of it. The value of religious rituals depends on the effects they have on a person. Religious rituals enhance a person when they strengthen worthwhile values or beliefs, or offer opportunities for religious experiences that help him toward fulfillment. Religious experience seems to have been downplayed in the larger, more organized churches of the West, but the contemporary quest for self-awareness reminds us that ecstatic experience has an honored place in religious traditions and should be part of our modern religion too. The new awareness of man, his needs, and his search for fulfillment has been reflected in morality. Religious morality today is one that recognizes cultural limitations, is orientated toward man's fulfillment, and insists on personal responsibility.

Chapter 5

Organized Religion

When an individual belongs to a church, it is difficult to draw a clean line between his personal religion and the religious structure to which he belongs. In the preceding chapters we have tried to focus on the individual; now we are shifting the focus to take in the corporate structure of the church. What follows applies equally well to a church considered on a universal level, such as all of Islam; to a local church, for example, a parish; or to a religious order in a church. Each of these is a religious organization.

The examination of institutions is necessary in addition to the examination of individuals because institutions are more than the sum of the individuals within them. No one would equate an automobile with a ton of assorted metals, glass, and plastic. When the parts are organized the overall structure has characteristics quite unlike any of the parts. Groups generate psychological characteristics that individuals do not have. For example, once there is a group, pressures toward conformity arise. Conformity is a psychological trait that can exist only in groups. Similarly, groups tend to generate anonymity. When an individual is the decision-maker, he is obviously responsible, but when a group makes a decision, responsibility is harder to pinpoint because the group members do not concur equally in the decision or contribute equally to the decision-making process. The psychological study of mobs reveals how different a person can be when he is part of a crowd from when he is alone. Clearly, then, to the study of individuals must be added the study of organizations.

Why Have Churches?

Many persons are content to be religious without belonging to churches—maybe because of a strong personal need for religious individuality, or maybe because they were brought up outside church structures and never felt a need for them, or maybe because they once belonged to a church and found no significant benefit in membership. They seem to be no less good or fulfilled than church members. Still, there are advantages in religious organization which these people may experience in other kinds of groups or in less formal ways.

Perhaps the most important advantage in church membership is the sharing of values and meaning. Churches are teachers. They transmit meanings for life and the values that people have found essential for their fulfillment. Not only do the churches frequently take the task of introducing meanings and values to the young if parents fail to do so, but they also continue to reinforce these meanings and values throughout the entire lifespan of the individual. As a group the church exerts conformity pressures that lead persons to share the same feelings, behaviors, and thought patterns as the other group members. As long as the "mind of the group" is itself conducive to personal fulfillment, the conformity forces are advantageous. Of course, we are speaking here not of a forced, compulsory conformity, which would frustrate the fulfillment of the individual as an autonomous person, but of the conformity deliberately chosen because it is a conformity to genuine values for personal fulfillment.

As teachers, the churches should also help the individual to continually reassess the meanings and values that are transmitted. Within the church as a group will be found perceptive and thought-provoking members who help the others to shed inadequate notions and to grow continuously. Thus the church member may find it easier than the non-church-member to get beyond the religion of childhood to a mature religious orientation.

Churches also offer advantages in terms of political and economic power. Undeniably this power has been, and sometimes still is, used by churches to force themselves or their distinct values on a society. Nearly everyone can find some causes espoused by churches that he agrees with and some causes he disagrees with. The person who objects to Catholic power in Spain or Protestant power in Northern Ireland might be in favor of the involvement of some of the U.S. churches in civil rights or in welfare legislation. Unless a person uses religion as an escape from responsibility by cultivating a leave-it-to-God attitude, he is bound to be concerned about the injustices within a society. The concerned individual, however, is relatively impotent compared to an organized group of concerned people.

Not too long ago there appeared in the *New York Times* a full-page advertisement paid for by laymen of various churches protesting the involvement of their denominations in social issues. They were calling for the churches to rid themselves of all interests other than preaching the word of God. In the past churches have always done more than preach. Institutions like schools, hospitals, and orphanages were originally nurtured primarily by churches and only later taken over by public, secular agencies. Churches often seem to be bolder than governments in undertaking new social enterprises. Even if one argues that churches should back out of social areas once adequate secular systems have been developed, the churches would still be engaged in social issues, for it is their particular penchant frequently to spot a society's needs and weaknesses before the society as a whole is ready to do anything about them.

The Western churches of today function in society precisely opposite to the way the churches of the medieval and early modern period moved. In the Middle Ages and in the centuries immediately following the Reformation, the churches were the stabilizing and homogenizing forces in society. They were closely allied with governments and preserved the *status quo*. They discouraged change. As a matter of fact, the churches continued to favor the old monarchical governments even after the people overthrew them. Nowadays the churches see themselves more as critics and agitators whose function is to encourage the changes that seem necessary in society. Thus it is to society as well as to individuals that churches offer advantages.

Thought and Discussion: (1) What sort of conformity pressures operate in your church? (2) Do many parents leave it to the church to give their children meaning for life and values? (3) Is your church, on the local level, involved or not involved in social issues? Why? (4) Does your church tend more to preserve the *status quo* or to initiate social change?

Change in Churches

Churches, like individuals, grow only by changing. Although less commonly now than ten years ago, many people still expect churches to be unchanging institutions, sometimes because they believe these institutions are divine and perfect. But most church members feel their church could be a little bit better in some ways. They would like to see some changes. In the past, when a large percentage of a church's members felt that some changes were necessary and another large percentage did not feel so, the result was a schism. Consequently we find Judaism split into orthodox, liberal, and conservative segments, and Christianity split into Protestant and Catholic segments.

The tendency to break up in times of great change seems conspicuously absent today, possibly because the mass media give people a better knowledge of what is happening in their churches. Although general attitudes toward churches are more critical, people do not expect their churches to be perfect. The radical changes in Catholicism during the last decade have seriously alienated a small conservative group of the church's membership while pleasing many more. The few well-known Catholic clergymen and theologians who left the church recently were people who had held exaggerated, idealistic notions of the church as an impeccable institution and so were greatly disillusioned when the church's shortcomings were thrust upon them by the mass media or by their own experiences in the church.

In today's world, no institution can hide its imperfections. At the opening of the Second Vatican Council, Pope John XXIII overturned the onesided scholarship of many a Catholic historian when he acknowledged that the Catholic church had failed in some ways and was partly to blame for the Catholic-Protestant schism in Christianity. He said that the church must reform itself, and this came as a jolt to those theologians who had said that the church was incapable of reform because it was divinely guided to perfection. Pope

John XXIII gave Catholics a new view of their church, more consistent with what people could see for themselves. This new view generated more tolerant attitudes both in non-Catholics and in Catholics themselves. Catholics who see failures of one sort or another in their church no longer feel they must leave the church. They can accept shortcomings in the church and stay with it.

The "mind of a group" is generally somewhat primitive and far below the intelligence of its individual members, as illustrated by the gullibility and impulsive behavior of crowds. It is not surprising, then, that in churches, like other institutions, new learning comes about most easily through new patterns of behavior. As in the case of a small child, something is done or experienced first and understood later. When the U.S. wanted to integrate black and white soldiers in the army, preliminary surveys revealed very hostile attitudes among the soldiers; but after the integration was actually carried out by command, follow-up studies showed great tolerance. Similarly, a major survey of Catholics in the diocese of Worcester, Massachusetts, showed that while the Catholics who had experienced in their parishes the changes brought about by Vatican II greatly favored them, Catholics in parishes where renewal had not been implemented were generally opposed to the changes they heard about.

Perhaps the group's intellectual resistance to change is linked to another primitive characteristic of the collective mind, namely, its lack of a time sense. The past is only a smudge reaching back from the present to the time when God created. Small children cannot imagine a time when the world was without television and automobiles; they presume that the past was just like the present. The collective mind of a group also tends to exhibit this infantile lack of a historical sense. The beliefs, activities, and structures of the group are believed to go back to the very origins of the group. Church members are liable to think that their beliefs and customs go all the way back to the time when the church was founded, maybe even to some divine origin. Catholics often think that their church was always the way it is today. They find it hard to imagine that for the first several centuries their priests were married, their bishops were elected by the people, their Mass had no fixed form, there were disagreements about what writings should be included in the Sacred Scriptures, and so on. Change is difficult when a group has no historical awareness.

When a group does have some concept of the past, it is apt to be a naive, mythical notion of a golden age, like an old man's memory of his childhood days. Christians imagine the thousands of martyrs who died for their faith before the roaring crowds in the Colosseum, although historians have their doubts about whether a single Christian ever died in that particular amphitheater. It can be exasperating for a Christian reading the history of the early councils to find that church dogmas were sometimes decided, not by theological reasoning in the councils, but by street fights between the private armies of the bishops, and that in the eleventh century one council finally passed a law requiring that henceforward all bishops coming to council meetings must leave their swords at the city gates. *The Acts of the Apostles*, the earliest history of church, which is accepted as part of the Sacred Scriptures of the New Testament, reveals that from the beginning there was within the church prejudice, controversy, scandals, and uncertainties. When a church is considering change, it makes little sense to talk about a return to its original form or to take its original form as the guide for change. What an organization must be faithful to is the present.

As churches pass through historical development, like

the life stages of an individual, there are three important periods to be distinguished. The first is the period of live revelation when the church believes that God is speaking through its members. At this point, there is great diversity in the church as many different viewpoints exist side by side. Changes occur rapidly and are readily accepted.

The second stage comes when it is felt that there have been too many changes and there is too much diversity in the group. Thus the first stage is ended and the second stage begun when it is declared that the period of revelation is over. The religion now becomes a "book religion" in the sense that it bases itself on writings of past revelations and discredits any new ideas. Judaism reached this point in the fifth century B.C. when the reformer Esdras announced that the age of prophecy was over. In Christianity it came at the end of the fourth century when it was decided that revelation ended with the death of the last apostle. A period of consolidation and centralization follows. Diversities are eliminated and beliefs are standardized, so that the result is a homogenized church.

The third stage slowly evolves from the second. It is the stage during which all the members of the church come to believe that the homogenized church was the original church. The past is idealized; present structures are regarded as divine and unchangeable. Thus the church becomes entrapped in a particular culture. At this point the church must either undergo a rebirth or a slow decay.

Thought and Discussion: (5) Do you believe that your church can fail? (6) The survey of Catholics in Worcester revealed that most of them did not know what the Second Vatican Council was. What do you know about the Council? Did this Council really do anything significant? (7) In what ways is your church changing? Why are changes being made? Are changes too slow or too fast in your church? (8) What are the advantages and disadvantages of a "book religion" based on Scripture? Was your church originally a "book religion"?

Church Structures and Individuals

The relationship between the organization and the individual is not the same in every church. In some churches the organization has little authority, and the individual member enjoys a wide range of options in his beliefs and behaviors. In other churches the organization holds great authority, and the individual is considerably restricted in what he may believe and how he may behave. In their organizational structures churches also reflect the cultures in which they exist as well as the goals they set for themselves.

The key to a church's structure is the amount of power invested in the clergy. Churches have always been faced with the question of what role the clergy should have. At the very beginning of Judaism, according to the Old Testament book of Deuteronomy, some Israelites challenged Moses for establishing a priesthood under the leadership of his brother Aaron. The fact that the book of Deuteronomy was edited by Jewish priests centuries later as a defense of their priesthood suggests that the issue remained a live one right up to the time when the Temple of Jerusalem was destroyed by the Babylonians. Similarly, the New Testament gives some evidence of nepotism in the early Christian church in Jerusalem; and the Gospel of St. Mark, written by St. Peter's loyal secretary, contains vigorous arguments for giving the clergy a rank high over other believers.

One of the most significant changes effected by the Protestant reformers in their churches was diminishing the clergy's role. In Protestantism, as in Judaism, the clergy is responsible to the local congregation. It was so in early Christianity too, but when in the course of history the local churches fell under the control of feudal lords who wanted to dictate church policies, the bishop of Rome began taking more and more power to himself to appoint clergy from the outside. Now that in many countries there is no longer any political control over the local churches, there are some stirrings in Catholicism toward restoring a fraction of the local church's voice in naming its clergy.

Until very recently Catholicism in the U.S. was a ghetto church. Most of the large immigrant groups—the Irish, the Italians, the Polish, the Puerto Ricans, the Mexicans—were poor and uneducated people. Their clergy, however, were highly educated. It was quite natural for these people to lean heavily on their clergy for leadership in secular as well as religious affairs. As such immigrant groups work their way into the mainstream of society and raise their own level of education, their dependence on the clergy decreases. Now among the more established groups, the laity equal the clergy in education and as a consequence are asking for more voice in their churches. The Second Vatican Council made it mandatory for parishes to have councils of laymen as part of their governmental structures, although the role of such councils was not specified.

Along with historical and cultural factors, the goals of a church influence its structure. In this century Protestantism has experienced a need for more centralization in some ways. The World Council of Churches is the outgrowth of various movements to pool resources for more effective church work, both in missions and at home. Enterprises which call for the involvement of the churches are sometimes too large for a local church or even a denomination to be effective. In the U.S., Protestants, Catholics, and Jews have jointly formed the United Council of Churches to respond to mutual concerns. While seeking common goals, these churches steadfastly maintain their individual traditions. Any talk of a super-church into which all will blend is out of the question. True ecumenism does not necessarily eliminate differences but respects them.

Within the individual church also there are some indications that diversity is an attribute to be prized. Where there is little diversity, there may be little genuine religion. It has been shown, for example, that race prejudice is more prevalent among regular church-goers than in non-church members. It is not that going to church increases prejudice, and the churches do preach the opposite. But prejudice is usually found in the more conforming, authoritarian type of person who tends to be attracted to churches because these institutions also place a high value on conformity and authority. These people agree with the other church members, but their religion has little effect on their deeper attitudes or feelings. High levels of conformity are made possible by low levels of personal conviction.

Conformity among believers is possible only if they do not integrate religion into their individual personality structures. Once believers start to bring their own perceptions and life experiences into their religion, differences between them start to appear. Within themselves today the churches can sense more and more diversity among their members. In a fluid society where people move from one class to another and from one neighborhood to another, they are less likely to hold onto their religion, associated as it is with one's nationality, social status, or neighborhood. Personal conviction is much more important, and the more personal one's religion is, the more likely he is to differ from other church members. It seems neither possible nor healthy for a church to expect all its members to be the same in all aspects of their religion.

Thought and Discussion: (9) Does the individual in your church have enough freedom to be different? (10) What role does the clergy play in your church? Does the clergy have too much control over the laity? Does the laity have too much control over the clergy? (11) What is the role of the laity in your church? (12) Is your church in need of more or less centralization?

Healthy and Unhealthy Church Structures

It is surely an oversimplification to speak of a church as healthy or unhealthy because, although a church may lean a little more in one direction than in the other, the same church is likely to be healthy in some ways and unhealthy in others. We take for granted that a church exists for the benefit of its members. To the extent that a church helps its members find fulfillment, it is healthy. To the extent that a church frustrates its members, it is unhealthy.

The first way a church can be healthy or not is in its cultural orientation. The unhealthy church is one that is embedded in a foreign culture, either the culture of a previous era or the culture of another part of the world. To endure over centuries or to be transplanted from one society to another and still remain vital, a religion has to be changed. Missionaries are most aware of this necessity. In religious rituals for weddings and funerals, for example, the symbolism of the colors black and white is reversed as one goes from a European culture to an African culture. The phrase in the Christian creed that Jesus "sits at the right hand of the Father" would baffle an oriental for whom the place of honor is on the left. For centuries the fourth commandment was interpreted to include supporting elderly parents; this might no longer make any sense in some socialist countries where they are well provided for. The medieval belief that it was sinful to charge interest on a loan would wreck modern Western society. Churches must obviously be free to adjust to changing cultures.

A religion should help a person to understand and live in his world, not in some other world. Some of the more obvious alien ghetto churches in the U.S. seem to nurture social barriers between their members and the rest of society, to the detriment of their members, who are impressed with how different they are. The feeling of being different easily glides into the feeling of being inferior and of being scorned, and thence into a multitude of mass social neuroses. Apart from positively severing a person from the culture in which he must live, however, a church can fail by simply being an irrelevant ghost from another culture. The healthy church is one that sheds light on the present culture and helps its members find fulfillment in it.

A second way a church may be healthy or not is in the service of all its members. Some churches tend to serve certain members exceedingly well while ignoring others. One instance is American Catholicism, which has often been described as a child's church. The great bulk of the church's resources are poured out for the children, while the adults in the church are merely regarded as the children's parents. Recently there has been much talk of shifting the educational emphasis in American Catholicism from the children to the parents, but usually with the same intent to serve one group and ignore the other. In the area of economic differences, churches of the same denomination have hardly begun to bridge the differences between their rich parishes and their poor ones. Little need be said of churches that separate the congregation according to race. A healthy church is one that brings its members together and attends to the needs of all.

A third way in which a church may be healthy or not is in its religious class structure. Some churches are like South American societies with enormous populations of second class members and just a few first class members. The latter control the religion; they are the clergy and the theologians. They alone are considered competent to understand the religion and govern the church. Historians of religion have noted that defunct religions in their dying stages had rituals that only the clergy could perform, beliefs that only the clergy could understand, and moral laws that only the clergy could interpret.

On the other hand, there are churches with a religious class structure more like American and European society with a large middle class of members who understand their religion and participate in the continuous evolution of their church. The members are not regarded as people to be led and taught by a few others but as co-believers equally in touch with God and equally capable of distinguishing adequate from inadequate religious notions.

Finally, a church may be healthy or not in its internal communications; that is, the church may be more or less aware of what the members are thinking and experiencing. The self-awareness of a church, to some extent, is conditioned by its structure. The church of two extreme classes of believers—all-knowing clergy versus ignorant laity—is much more subject to communication gaps than the church of co-believers. Where the communications gap is extreme, we have the schizophrenic church that is officially saying one thing while its members believe something else. When the church regards its members as competent believers who can participate in the continuous growth and renewal of the church, more self-awareness and more internal consistency in the church result. With modern social research techniques, it is much easier for churches, if they wish, to discover what their members really believe. So far it has generally been left up to outside agencies, such as magazines and newspapers, to study the church. The results have been little patches of sometimes unimportant data. Surely all the churches would be more healthy if they used the available means to increase their self-awareness as groups.

Thought and Discussion: (13) Does your church help you to understand the culture in which you live and find fulfillment in it? (14) Does your local church serve all its members or are some groups privileged and others ignored? (15) What kind of religious class structure does your church have? (16) Does your church have effective internal communications?

Reformers

If churches are to be effective in reforming individuals and societies, it is only natural that they should experience reform within themselves. Reform is not likely to be brought about by outside agencies. Churches, like other organizations, give little weight to the critiques of non-members. Views from the outside are readily dismissed as prejudiced or ill-informed. Reformers must come from within the church.

The greatest religious reformer of recent times was Pope John XXIII. Although this seemingly simple old man was elected to the papacy as an interim pope who was expected just to keep the office filled for a few years until a more suitable candidate could be agreed on, his very lack of sophistication enabled him to be a successful reformer. It seemed out of place when the newspapers of the world carried a picture of a smiling Pope with a cigarette in his hand. It also seemed out of place when he said that the church, so intent on reforming the world, itself needed to be reformed. He was no fiery zealot. He did not have to be. More important, he was in touch with the thoughts and feelings of ordinary people. His concern was not for his own prestige or power but for the good of his church's members. Although he was old and did not live long enough to see his reformation through, he initiated the trends toward change in Catholicism that continue unabated.

The successful leader of a group is not necessarily a man of new ideas, but he is the person who senses what the group members are already thinking. He is able to bring their thinking out into the open. Pope John XXIII's success as a reformer was not based on any theological skill. He left the theology to others. He saw, however, the thoughts and feelings that lay restless in the minds and hearts of the church's members, and he brought them into the open with a blessing. His reformation could not be reversed because it was the surfacing of long-simmering sentiments, not a quick program.

Perhaps it was the pageantry and international religious politics of the Second Vatican Council that first whetted the appetites of the mass media. No matter what started it, the interests of the press in the churches speedily spiraled, and a highly developed religious journalism resulted. Religious journalism has so mushroomed that everyone now knows what happens in the churches. Even new theological ideas are immediately available for public examination. Churches can no longer "protect" their members from knowing about church politics or about new theological notions. The consequence may be that we shall have no more great reformers.

Instead the church as a whole may be its own reformer. With the entire membership well-informed, a church can be guided by the consensus of its members.

Still, churches will have their individual critics. A church without critics in its ranks is likely to stagnate. In the Old Testament we find critics of the established religion holding a preeminent place. Jeremiah said that the sign of a true prophet is that he speaks more woe than weal while the false prophet keeps saying that everything is fine. From the Old Testament, however, we also learn that the true prophet is generally unwelcome in his church and often punished for his criticisms. In anticipating his own death, the Jewish reformer Jesus reminded his hearers of the violent deaths of the great Old Testament prophets.

The person who would be a reformer today must bring about renewal by educating the members of his church so that they become aware of what changes are necessary. Even in a very authoritarian church the consensus of the members will eventually prevail. The churches recognize that the search for fulfillment is a common venture which the members undertake together. The church whose members were taught to pray, pay, and obey is vanishing. Today's church members have something to say. The breath of God is stirring up the members of the church and, like the dry bones of Ezekiel's vision, they are rising up as living beings. The future of the church is in their hands.

Thought and Discussion: (17) Who are the critics in your church today? How does the church regard them? (18) On the local level does your church have any viable structure, such as open parish meetings, for people to express their views on what is happening, or not happening, in the church? (19) How has the increase in religious journalism affected your faith

as an individual? (20) In practical terms how can a church be
guided by the consensus of its members?

Summary

Institutions have profound effects on individuals.
Churches help individuals to share values and meaning. They
also teach and help the individual in his growing. Unlike
the church of the Middle Ages which was wed to the *status
quo*, the contemporary churches act as agents of change in
society. Not only are the churches expected to exert pressures for change in the world, but also they are expected to
change themselves. A clear awareness of its history and a belief that God is speaking today are essential for the progress
of the church. The mass media and general education have
produced a concerned and knowledgeable laity in recent
years. More individuality is evident among church members.
The church has to be aware of how the culture is affecting
it and its members. Churches should serve all their members
and be attentive to the voices of all. The reform that has
been taking place in Catholicism since the time of Pope John
XXIII has been effective because it corresponds to what people
feel about the church and hope for in the church. In an age
of mass communications, individual critics may be less significant than the body of the church as a whole, but critics will
continue to be necessary for the growth of the church toward
the ultimate kingdom.

SELECTED BIBLIOGRAPHY

Chapter 1: RELIGIOUS DEVELOPMENT

David Elkind. "The Development of Religious Understanding in Children and Adolescents." In *Research on Religious Development*, edited by M.P. Stromen. New York: Hawthorne Books, 1971.

Ronald Goldman. *Readiness for Religion*. New York: Seabury Press, 1965.

R.J. Havighurst and B. Keating. "The Religion of Youth." In *Research on Religious Development*, edited by M.P. Stromen. New York: Hawthorne Books, 1971.

P.B. Maves. "Religious Development in Adulthood." In *Research on Religious Development*, edited by M.P. Stromen. New York: Hawthorne Books, 1971.

Chapter 2: WHY PEOPLE ARE RELIGIOUS

Andrew Greeley. *Unsecular Man: A Persistence of Religion*. New York: Schocken, 1972.

A.M. Greeley and P.H. Rossi. *The Education of Catholic Americans*. Garden City, New York: Doubleday Anchor, 1968.

Ignace Lepp. *Atheism in Our Time*. New York: Macmillan, 1964.

Philip E. Slater. *Microcosm: Structural, Psychological and Religious Evolution in Groups*. New York: John Wiley and Sons, 1966.

Charles W. Stewart. *Adolescent Religion: A Developmental Study of the Religion of Youth*. Nashville: Abingdon Press, 1967.

Chapter 3: RELIGION AND PERSONALITY

Gordon W. Allport. *The Individual and His Religion.* New York: Macmillan, 1960.

Gregory Baum. *Man Becoming: God in Secular Experience.* New York: Herder and Herder, 1970.

R.J. Becker. "Religion and Psychological Health." In *Research on Religious Development,* edited by M.P. Stromen. New York: Hawthorne Books, 1971.

Abraham H. Maslow. *Toward a Psychology of Being.* Princeton, New Jersey: D. van Nostrand, 1962.

Rollo May. *Man's Search for Himself.* New York: Signet, 1953.

Chapter 4: MATURE RELIGION

W.H. Clark. "Intense Religious Experience." In *Research on Religious Development.* New York: Hawthorne, 1971.

Charles Curran, ed. *Absolutes in Moral Theology?* Washington: Corpus Books, 1968.

John J. Heaney, ed. *Faith, Reason, and the Gospels.* Westminster, Maryland: Newman Press, 1965.

William James. *The Varieties of Religious Experience.* New York: Mentor Books, 1958.

Orlo Strunk. *Mature Religion.* Nashville: Abingdon, 1965.

Chapter 5: ORGANIZED RELIGION

Roland H. Bainton. *The Age of the Reformation.* Princeton, New Jersey: D. van Nostrand, 1956.

Erik H. Erikson. *Young Man Luther.* New York: W.W. Norton and Co., 1958.

Andrew Greeley. *What a Modern Catholic Believes About the Church.* Chicago: Thomas More, 1972.

Adrian van Kaam. *Personality Fulfillment in the Religious Life.* Wilkes-Barre, Pennsylvania: Dimension Books, 1967.